Toward a Theology of Beauty

John Navone, S.J.

A Liturgical Press Book

The Liturgical Press
Collegeville, Minnesota

Cover design by Fred Petters. *The Crucifixion* by Georges Rouault, The Minneapolis Institute of Arts, Minneapolis, Minnesota.
Used with permission.

The Scripture quotations contained herein are the author's translation.

 Printed in the United States of America.

1 2 3 4 5 6 7 8

Library of Congress Cataloging-in-Publication Data

Navone, John J.
Toward a theology of beauty / John Navone.
p. cm.
Includes bibliographical references.
ISBN 0-8146-2272-0
1. Aesthetics—Religious aspects—Christianity. 2. God—Beauty. 3. Beatific vision. I. Title.
BR115.A838 1996
231′.4—dc20

96-2624
CIP

Contents

Introduction

Christian theology, based on the historical revelation that God is the Creator of all things, assumes that we can know the truth, and love the goodness, and delight in the beauty of all things because the Creator first knows and loves and delights in all creation. The Creator, Happiness Itself, knows truth and loves goodness and delights in beauty; consequently, whatever proceeds from the Creator—all creation—is knowable, lovable, and enjoyable. In the loving gaze of contemplation we can, therefore, "see" the Creator in the truth and goodness and beauty of all things. We can have communion with Happiness Itself in knowing and loving and delighting in all things.

That we are the image and likeness of the Creator is another basic datum of divine revelation. If creation/creativity is at the heart of beauty, so too the splendor and clarity of form. Humankind, formed in the image and likeness of the Creator, was beautifully conformed, in loving obedience, to the will/love and wisdom of the Creator. When humankind turned away, in self-will, from the Creator, it lost its beautiful conformity; the human image was deformed. Christ, the new Adam, is the perfect image/form of God, conformed in loving obedience to the Creator who has sent him to transform/transfigure the deformed image of the Creator. Beauty Itself makes all humankind beautiful in and through its perfect form/image. We contemplate Beauty Itself in the crucified and glorified/risen Christ.

The Christian community of faith recognizes in Jesus Christ the power of Beauty Itself to inspire, motivate, transform, and shape human life. The Creator, Beauty Itself, seizes and enraptures humankind when manifested in perfect form, the crucified and glorified Christ. Beauty Itself draws us to Itself in fulfillment of Christ's promise: "When I am lifted up (crucified), I shall draw everyone to myself." In the loving contemplation of the crucified, the community of faith sees that God is Love: Beauty Itself. It recognizes the saving power of Beauty to communicate the fullness of life.

Jesus' farewell discourse offers another datum for a theology of beauty. Jesus explains that he goes gladly to his glorification in giving his life for all humankind so that the joy of his life in God, in Beauty Itself, might become ours. Eternal happiness is the beatific vision of Beauty Itself/Love Itself. In the light of that Love, all is lovely; in the light of that Beauty, all is beautiful. The fullness of life is the fullness of love and delight in Beauty Itself. The self-giving love of Beauty Itself, revealed in the invincible love of the crucified and risen Christ, draws us to itself in the true beauty of all things, the gift and call of the Creator to eternal delight in the fullness of life/love.

In contrast to *true* beauty, the allure of all that attracts us to our ultimate happiness and fulfillment, *seductive* beauty is the allure of all that entices us to our ultimate unhappiness and destruction. The distinction between true and false friends, true and apparent goods, is analogous. Both the prudent and the clever know the means they must choose to attain their ends; however, the prudent achieve moral excellence and self-fulfillment, and the clever tend towards their moral self-destruction. True beauty is always the source of joy and delight in whatever draws us to our true and eternal happiness in Beauty/Happiness Itself.

If we cannot live without happiness, as Aristotle claimed, we cannot live without beauty. If happiness is the epitome of all that we are incapable of not willing, we desire the beauty of that love which delights us. Joy and happiness are our reponse to partaking of something we love; and if loving, simple approval, is something beloved in itself, then our desire for happiness can be satisfied by such affirmation directed toward another; that is, by unselfish love. We rejoice in the radiant manifestation of love that is beauty. The essence of love consists in shared joy and happiness, indispensable goods of life which can be enjoyed only by their being "given" to us; for the beauty/love that gives joy and happiness is always free and unconstrained. Infatuation, erotic love kindled first and foremost by physical beauty—only one aspect of personal beauty—is always a form of bondage; it is not love. At best, it is the beginning of love.

True lovers cannot conceal their joy; they actually radiate the beauty of their shared joy and happiness. Beauty discloses or radiates the truth and goodness of things; therefore, it entails communication, communion, and community.

When the senses no longer observe beauty and the intellect can no longer detect any meaning or value, what ultimately sustains love and remains believable as its real justification is the conviction that everything is a creature, creatively willed, affirmed, loved by the Creator and for that reason really good/beautiful and therefore susceptible to, but also worthy of, being loved by us. Charity, a love for God that loves God as the object and author of all happiness, enables us to contemplate the truth and goodness and beauty of the Creator in all things with joyful gratitude for all things. Charity enables the true vision of all as gift from the loving creator, irradiating that joy which lasts forever.

We cannot separate Beauty Itself from its mystery. We cannot separate the comprehensible from the incomprehensible, the communicable from the incommunicable. We know Beauty Itself in the mystery of the divine, that is to say the total complex of mysteries which are revealed and are radically one in the mystery of Christ. Secondly, we know Beauty Itself in the mystery of the I-Thou relationship, of my being a person in relation to the personal being of others. We know the mystery of the beautiful in the mystery of the Absolute Being who is at the same time the Interpersonal Triune Absolute and the Absolute Beauty. Beauty and happiness are given to us independently of our appetites and desires. Both entail an enjoyment, a love, of what transcends our very appetites and desires.

Christian theologians are engaged upon the task of articulating the *givenness* of life and selfhood, the experience of life and self as being grace. They view images in themselves secular as types which mediate the mystery of the dawn of God's kingdom, as epiphanies or manifestations of grace. Insofar as theologians open our eyes to the mysteriousness of all that is, they are activating and strengthening in us the capacity to rest in contemplation of the incomprehensible beauty of Beauty Itself. They are engaged upon mediating to us something of the mystery which we shall enjoy forever. They recall us from the forgetfulness of, and alienation from, the everyday but real revelation of the beauty and loveliness of God. Every true theologian seeks to communicate the incommunicable by articulating everyone's orientation to the One, the True, the Good, and the Beautiful. The theologians, like the poets, are concerned not merely with the imparting of abstract formulations but seek to share their living experience with others. Like St. John they speak of the Word of Life so that they may have union with their hearers and that their own joy may be complete (1 John 1:1). Theologians are engaged in a dialogue, not only with their public, but with the object of their contemplation. The blessing which is heaven is not the satisfaction of our finite questions by finite answers; it is rather the ignorance of the wise where our hearts find rest in the incomprehensibility of Beauty Itself, which is perceived without the aid of concepts. It is not a body of rationally reflected knowledge but an experience of the interplay of unity, truth, and goodness. It is Being perceived as a whole independently of its analysis into the true and the good. Just as enjoying a beautiful piece of music or painting brings us into contact with the unknowable mystery of Being, so too heaven remains a resting in mystery, a knowing in ignorance, an enjoyment of that which transcends our very appetites.

Rahner has argued that the experience of self, an experience which is not only anterior to every other experience, but which is also the very condition of the possibility of all other experiences, is a unity with, though not of course identical with, the experience of God or Beauty Itself. Our openness to the transcendent, our orientation to mystery, implies for Rahner a real though nonthematic experience of God. By nonthematic Rahner means something neither expressed nor expressible in concepts or categories (see his "Experience of Self and Experience of God," *Theological Investigations* [London, 1975] 13:122–32). If Rahner is correct, and the very possibility of consciousness implies a primordial though wordless experience of God, the articulation of our deepest experience will always in some sense be a theology, albeit not necessarily explicit and formalized. By God's gift to me of my humanity, I have, prior to every thought, feeling, or wish, an awareness of myself which precedes my ability to think in concepts. This awareness implies an equally nonconceptual awareness of Beauty Itself as the horizon in which I do my knowing and willing. Awareness of my limitations, however nonthematic, implies an awareness of the Unlimited. Awareness of my relativity, be it never so unreflected upon, implies an awareness of the Absolute. It is an awareness of Truth and Goodness and Beauty which precedes and makes possible every subsequent act of understanding the true or willing the good or enjoying the beautiful.

Pythagoras, Plato, and Plotinus described beauty as the eternal splendor of the One showing through the Many: in the many different forms in our universe, the One shines through and gives splendor and meaning to all reality. Aristotle understood beauty in terms of harmony: the condition when everything fits; when, in a scientific theory or the Parthenon, one has the conviction that nothing could be added or subtracted. All the parts are in harmony with all the other parts.

Plato, when considering the triad of beauty, truth, and goodness, gave the first place to beauty because it is harmony, and whether truth or goodness are harmonious is the test of their integrity. Plato believed that ethical goodness consists of acting in a way that is harmonious with other human beings. In fact, the Greek word for beauty and for goodness is the same *(kalon).*

Beauty is the mystery that enchants and delights; it engenders a sense of joy and peace. Rollo May calls attention to the exhilarating impact of beauty as the splendor of the truth that speaks out to all who listen patiently: "Nobel Laureate in physics, Heisenberg pointed out that the researcher in physics recognizes truth by the splendor of its beauty" (*My Quest For Beauty* [Dallas: Saybrook, 1985] 29).

Beauty Itself creates, sustains, and draws to perfection the whole of creation. All created beauty reflects and participates in the splendor of Beauty Itself; it is perceived without the aid of concepts, independently of its analysis into the good and the true. The beauty of creation in the light of Jesus Christ, Beauty Itself incarnate, inspires/grounds our theology/spirituality of beauty.

The basic assumption of this book is this: If God is Happiness Itself, communion with God is communion with Happiness Itself. If Happiness Itself is forever knowing its truth, and loving its goodness, and delighting in its beauty, our ultimate and eternal happiness in the gift of the beatific vision is communion with Happiness Itself, knowing its truth and loving its goodness and delighting in its beauty. The eye of faith that is love, even now in a glass darkly, enjoys something of that Beauty Itself which is a joy forever in the beatific vision. God's love flooding our hearts through the Holy Spirit given to us (Rom 5:5) is even now drawing us to the fullness of life in the kingdom of Happiness Itself, when we shall know ourselves in the splendor of God's truth, and love ourselves in the splendor of God's goodness, and delight in ourselves in the splendor of God's beauty.

1

Creation and the Beauty of All Things

We can affirm the truth and goodness and beauty of all things because they are created. When we make this affirmation, we are not speaking about something which we see and know for ourselves. Rather, we are relying on a divine revelation which can in no way be inferred or deduced from the empirical reality of the world and of humankind. In short, Christian theology is based on a divine revelation; it attempts to interpret the documents of that revelation preserved by the Christian tradition. The revelation that God is the Creator, the Origin and Ground and Destiny of all creation, is the ultimate basis for our affirming the truth (knowability) and goodness (lovability) and beauty (delightfulness) of all things. All things can be known and loved and enjoyed because they are created.[1]

Our belief in creation presupposes the communion of God's mind and the human mind—two knowing agents—in whatever is real. These "coordinates" place all reality between the absolutely creative, inventive knowledge of God and the imitating, "informed" knowledge of us humans and thus present the total realm of reality as a structure of interwoven original and reproduced conceptions. The concept of the truth of all things is based on this twofold orientation of all things as both thought by God and,

[1]This section is based largely on Josef Pieper's study of Thomistic thought in *Unaustrinkbares Licht* (Munich: Kösel-Verlag, 1963), translated by Lothar Krauth in *Josef Pieper: An Anthology* (San Francisco: Ignatius Press, 1981) 96–99.

therefore, knowable to the human mind. All things are true in the sense that they are known by God in the act of creation and are, therefore, by their nature accessible and comprehensible to the human mind.

The main cue we need to move toward an affirmation of God's existence, according to Bernard Lonergan, is found in the very knowability of the world.[2] For some reason, the world has a structure such that the human mind can penetrate it by means of its own processes of thought. How can we account for this fact? It might have been the case that human beings had intelligence but that the world was not amenable to exploration by that intelligence. There could have been a lack of fit between the world and the human mind. But in point of fact, there is not; on the contrary, there is considerable harmony between them as, among other things, the fruits of scientific knowledge in technology demonstrate. It is argued, therefore, that the world's intelligibility requires us to posit the existence of a creative mind, analogous to but infinitely transcending the human mind, by which the cosmos was brought into being.

All things can be known by us because they spring from God's thought. Because they originate in God's mind, things have not only their specific essence in themselves and for themselves, but precisely because they originate in God's mind, they have as well an essence for us. All things are intelligible, translucent, clear, and open because they are created by God's thought, and are therefore essentially spirit-related. The clarity and lucidity that flows from God's knowledge into things, together with/*as* their very being, makes all things knowable for the human mind. A thing has as much light as it has reality. The "reality" of a thing understood as "being created" is itself its light. Things can be known, loved, and enjoyed/delighted in because they are created by a knowing, loving, and enjoying/delightful Creator.

Our belief in creation presupposes an implicit communion of God and humankind in truly knowing and truly loving and truly enjoying/delighting in whatever is real. That the Creator has first known, loved, and delighted in all things endows all things with communicability as divinely and humanly knowable, lovable, and

[2]See H. Meynell, *The Intelligible Universe* (Totowa, N.J.: Barnes & Noble, 1982).

enjoyable. This is the twofold orientation of all things as divine gift and call for communion in knowing the truth, loving the goodness, and enjoying/delighting in the beauty of all things.

In the correlation between all things and the creative "knowing" of God lies the primordial and only "truth" of these things, a truth that in turn makes human knowledge at all possible. Our knowledge is the product of truth, flowing indeed from the truth of all things. The correlation between the reality of all nature and the prototypical creative "knowing" of God can never be formally known. We can know a thing but not its formal truth. We perceive a reproduction but not its correspondence to the original, not the correlation between the thoughts and its actualization. This correlation that primarily constitutes the formal truth of all things we cannot know. Here it becomes evident that being true and being unfathomable go together, and that the comprehensibility of a thing can never be fully exhausted by any finite mind—for all things are created, which means that the reason they are knowable (and lovable and enjoyable/delightful) is by necessity also the reason they are unfathomable.

"All things are true (and good and beautiful)" means primarily that all things are conceived by God. This assertion is not only about God and the divine action directed towards things, but also about the structure of things. It is another way of expressing Augustine's notion that things exist because God sees them, whereas we see things because they exist. It states that the existence and essence of things consists in their being conceived by the Creator. "True" is an ontological designation, a synonym for "real." Being and truth are interchangeable; it means the same when we say, "something conceived (loved, enjoyed/delighted in) by God." It is essential to all existing things as created to be modeled after an original idea that resides in the absolutely creative mind of God.

The correlation, however, between the original idea in God and its created reproduction, which formally and primarily constitutes the truth of all things, we can never directly apprehend. We cannot observe the emanation of things from God's mind. We cannot find a viewpoint that would allow us to compare the idea with its image. Consequently, our questing mind in its simplest things, falls short of its ultimate destination. This is because all things are created; their inner lucidity flows from their original idea in the infinitely radiant fullness of the Divine Mind.

The Creator contemplates both his first creation and his new creation with love. The Creator who affirms the goodness of his creation in Genesis affirms his love for his new creation, his Beloved (Son), in Mark's account of the baptism (1:11) and transfiguration (9:7) of Jesus. "Contemplation" means a *loving* gaze, the beholding of the beloved.[3] It expresses the way God sees God's self and all creation: with love and joy/delight. The world, as creation, is willed by God, which means that it is created *in love* and is therefore, by its mere existence, good. In the account of the new creation, the notion of God's delight/enjoyment is added. To enjoy a thing, on the other hand, is to make it the means to obtain what we enjoy. The Creator lovingly contemplates and enjoys his Beloved (Son) and all human persons without regard to usefulness. We are good in our Creator's delightfulness. The crucified and risen Christ reveals and communicates the Creator's self-giving love and joy for all who are called to be delightful friends rather than slaves (John 15:15). We exist because our Creator knows, loves, and enjoys us. We can be known, loved, and enjoyed because our Creator has first "thought," loved, and enjoyed us.

It is God who in the act of creation anticipated all conceivable human love and delight and said: I will you to be; it is good, "very good" (Gen 1:31) that you exist. God has already infused everything that human beings can love and affirm, goodness along with existence, and that means lovability and affirmability. Human love and delight, therefore, are by their nature and must inevitably always be an initiation and a kind of repetition of this creative love of God. And perhaps the lover is not unaware of this before reflecting at all; for even the first stirring of love and delight contains an element of gratitude, a kind of reply, knowing that one has been referred to something prior, in this case to a larger frame of universal reference which supersedes the realm of immediate empirical knowledge. All human love and delight are a kind of echo of the divine, creative, primary affirmation by virtue of which everything that is—including what we concretely love—has at once received existence and goodness and beauty. If all goes happily as it should, then in human love and delight something *more* takes place than mere echo, mere repeti-

[3] *Josef Pieper: An Anthology* (San Francisco, Ignatius Press, 1989) 120.

tion and imitation. What takes place is a continuation and in a certain sense even a perfecting of what was begun in the course of creation.

What matters to us, beyond mere existence, is how good and wonderful we find one another. The Creator, through the sustaining power of human love, continues and perfects our lives. To be loved and enjoyed by others is essential for our human development. For a child, and even for the still unborn child, being loved by the mother is the precondition for its own thriving. Our ability to love, in which our existence achieves its highest intensification, is preconditioned by our experience of being lovingly approved, cared for, and enjoyed. The song title "You're nobody 'til somebody loves you" captures the meaning of our Creator's love and its sustaining and fulfilling power in loving others. Such love affirms our meaning, goodness, and beauty. It is the matrix for grasping the proclamation of Christian faith that God is self-giving love and shows the power of such love to make all humankind the beautiful manifestation of that love.

Although there are countless reasons for joy and delight in the beauty of all things, there is one common denominator: possessing or receiving something we love. Consequently, one who does not love cannot rejoice, no matter how desperately one wishes to. If beauty, in its original meaning, is the splendor of the true and the good irradiating from every ordered state of being, it is not enjoyed/delighted in by one who fails to recognize/welcome that state of being.

If love means to rejoice in the perfection and goodness and happiness of another, our enjoyment of and delight in the true beauty of all things bespeaks our love for the infinitely good and supremely happy Creator of all things. It is tantamount to affirming and exclaiming: How good and wonderful that you exist! We share the joy and delight of the Creator in the relationship of love for the truth and goodness and beauty of all things. Such love and delight break through the principal isolation on which the whole philosophy of hell rests and so have gained a part, no matter how small, of "paradise." The indivisibility of love and joy derives from the indivisibility of goodness and beauty in the Creator. The glow of the true and the good irradiating from every ordered state of being is always the gift and call of Beauty Itself, of the loving and joyful Creator, to the fullness of life in communion. Beauty Itself calls us to be fully alive together with all others in that self-giving love and joy that lasts forever. The beauty of all things is even now a promise of that love and joy. It awakens our expectation of a beauty that no eye has yet seen nor ear heard (1 Cor 2:9).

Not only in the life to come but even now our happiness is only as great as our God-given capacity for contemplating the beauty of all things.[4] As creatures, we are designed for and desiring the vision of beauty. Not only does the act of vision beyond death exist in an inchoate form in this life, but also the object of that beatific vision can be glimpsed, however imperfectly, in the joy of contemplation. Because the world is a creature, God is present in it and able to reveal the divine self to the person whose attention is turned upon the depths of things. Only the vision of something we love makes us happy. Contemplation is a vision kindled by the act of turning towards something in love and affirmation. If we direct our loving power of affirmation towards the Creator, the infinite source of satisfaction which flows through

[4]Josef Pieper asserts that to the virtue of temperance as the preserving and defending realization of our inner order, the gift of beauty is particularly coordinated. Not only is temperance beautiful in itself, it also renders us beautiful. He bases his assertion on the original meaning of beauty as the glow of the true and the good irradiating from every ordered state of being, and not in the patient significance of immediate sensual appeal. The beauty of the temperance, he continues, has a more spiritual, austere, and virile aspect. On the other hand, Pieper asserts that the infantile disorder of intemperance destroys beauty. See Pieper, *The Four Cardinal Virtues,* trans. Richard and Clara Winston (New York: Harcourt, Brace & World, Inc., 1965) 203. Temperance or intemperance manifests itself in the order or disorder of our features, in our attitude and laugh. Temperance, as the inner order of a person, can as little remain purely interior as the soul itself, and as all other life of the soul or mind. It is the nature of the soul to be the form of the body. This fundamental principle of all Christian psychology, according to Pieper, not only states the informing of the body by the soul, but also the reference of the soul to the body. On this, a second factor is based: temperance or intemperance of outward behavior and expression can have its strengthening or weakening repercussion on the inner order of the person. It is from this point of view that all outer discipline—whether in the sphere of sexual pleasure or in that of eating or drinking, of self-assertion, of anger, and of the gratification of the eye, obtains its meaning, its justification, and its necessity (Ibid., 204).

all reality, and if this beloved source reveals itself to our gaze of the soul, then and only then occurs what can, in an absolute sense, be called contemplation. More positively, whenever these conditions are met, contemplation always occurs; for the blissful awareness of the divine satisfaction of all desire can be kindled by any event. In fact, it can be attained by one who does not even know the name of what is happening to oneself. Our delight in the basic truth and goodness and beauty of things is often an inconspicuous form of contemplation that is an authentic foretaste and beginning of perfect joy.[5] We can even now contemplate the Creator's loving face turned towards us in the truth and goodness and beauty of things; and, in the light of that face, we can see everything which is, is good, worthy of love, and loved by the Creator. We contemplate creation as reflecting and mediating the Creator's love.

The loving vision of the contemplative is true: it does not mistake the creature for the Creator, seeing it as an absolute, as absolutely necessary for my happiness. The true love and vision of the contemplative contrasts with the disordered love and distorted vision that mistakes the creature for the Creator. Like all idolatries and addictions, this love is blind and blinding.[6] God is love and God is not blind which means that the true love of the contemplative is not blind. The contemplative heart has its reasons; it sees the difference between the creature and the Creator, penetrating to the mysterious heart of what it loves and and delights in. It sees and loves and enjoys the Creator and creatures as they truly are: the Creator above all, and all creation under the sovereignty of the Creator's loving kindness. It sees that all is true and good and beautiful in the Creator's truth and goodness and beauty.[7]

[5]Josef Pieper, *Problems of Modern Faith,* trans. Jan van Heurck (Chicago: Herald Press, 1985) 150–51.

[6]Peter Kreeft, *God's Love* (Ann Harbor, Mich.: Servant Books, 1988) 34–35.

[7]God's knowledge and love are creative, not receptive. God does not know and love things because they exist; rather, they exist because God freely posits them—that is, knows and loves them as real. For us, the material finite universe is first in the order of knowing and loving; all our knowledge and love depend upon objectivity and receptivity; as the Scholastic dictum states, *nihil est in intellectu quod erat prius in sensu.* But God is absolute Subject; Mind

Beauty Itself and the Look of Love: The Joyous Contemplative Gaze of Divine and Human Love

Beauty Itself entails the joyful look of love, the joyous contemplative gaze of divine and human love. Mark's Gospel implies this link in his account of the baptism and transfiguration of Jesus where Jesus is recognized as the Beloved Son in whom God delights. Jesus irradiates the splendor of Beauty Itself on the Mount of the Transfiguration. The divine look of love glorifies Jesus, the Beloved Son; and the disciples rejoice in seeing the glory of God, the manifestation of the divine mind and heart and spirit.

Things are beautiful because their Creator is Beauty Itself; things are lovely because their Creator is Love Itself. We delight in the beauty and loveliness of all things because their Creator is Happiness Itself. All beauty/loveliness originates in and is for consciously knowing and loving subjects, divine and human. It is in them and for them before it is "out there."

Music offers an analogy of the spiritual nature of beauty. The delightfully beautiful music of Mozart is in Mozart before he writes it for a performance. Mozart possesses and enjoys the music in his mind and heart and imagination before anyone else can hear or enjoy it. When we finally do hear and enjoy his music we are truly enjoying Mozart. Analogously, whenever we delight in the beauty or loveliness of creation, we are implicitly delighting in their Creator, Happiness Itself.

Similarly our landscapes and townscapes reflect ourselves, our vision, and affectivity. There is probably no landscape that looks more loved, cherished, and cared for than that of Tuscany's

---

is first, not matter. Objects ultimately exist in reality because they are posited by absolute Mind or Spirit. God knows all in God's pure creative eternal act, which is identical with God's self. God knows things by consciously causing their existence. The existence of any thing is identical with its being caused by God. But all that God "does," God is; and all that God is, is conscious. Therefore God knows what God creates precisely in creating; or, put the other way around, God creates all things in knowing them. Furthermore, God does not create as a factor within the working of the world. God creates the whole as whole. The notion of God as "creator" distinguishes God's action from any other form of causality. See Richard Viladesau, *The Reason for Our Hope* (New York: Paulist Press, 1984) 170–71.

Chianti country, the greatest garden in Europe, part naturally made and part the work of human beings. History documents the look of love that this landscape irradiates. The formula for the investiture oath of the Chianti League, formed at the beginning of the fourteenth century for the administration and defense of the region, begins, "I promise to keep myself close to nature, to give a religious meaning to my life, to look around me with optimism and with love. . . ."[8]

The beauty of the Chianti landscape reflects both the divine and human inscape—the divine and human look of love—in communion.[9] It reminds us that the way in which we envision God

[8]Fulvio Roiter (photographs), Geno Pampaloni (text), Giosuè Chiaradia (notes), *Florence and Tuscany* (Udine: Magnus Edizioni, 1981), the notes for photos 147–49. No page numbers occur.

[9]Gerard Manley Hopkins (1844–89) was fascinated by those aspects of a thing, or group of things, which constitute its individually distinctive beauty. For this fundamental beauty which is the active principle of all true being, the source of all true knowledge and delight—even of religious ecstasy, he coined the word "inscape." The "inscape" of a being is the distinctive controlling energy that makes the being itself and connects it distinctively with all else. "Instress" is the action that takes place when the inscape of a given being fuses itself in a given human consciousness in contact at a given moment with the being. "Instress" brings this particular human self into the dynamics of the otherwise "objective" inscape. The given being possessing inscape and generating instress might be virtually anything: a brook, a woodlark, a farmer working a field, a piece of music, or a poem itself. Hopkins attends not only to the energy in the human interior but also to the energy concentrated in a given being or beings in the external world as well, that is, to the "inscape" within the object that catches our attention. For Hopkins, the "inscape" of a being, however individualized, moves outward by its "instress" to register in our cognitive-affective consciousness. All beings have a kind of outreach, and especially to human beings. The self that shares itself with others lives more fully in itself as well as in others. See W. H. Gardiner, *Poems and Prose of Gerard Manley Hopkins* (Baltimore: Penguin Books, 1963) xx–xxi; Walter J. Ong, *Hopkins, the Self, and God* (Toronto: University of Toronto Press, 1986) 17–18, 37–38, 45, 116.

The external world and the interior world of the self are not, for Hopkins, entirely separate. Walter J. Ong comments on this dimension of Hopkins' thought (Ibid., 156).

> Our bodies are both part of ourselves and part of the external world. In his sense of "inscape" and "instress" Hopkins finds the

is always determined from the start by the way we love and treasure the things presented to us within the context of our human life story.[10] Our concrete knowledge or vision of God is born of the love or lack of love with which we respond to the persons, places (townscapes and landscapes), and things, presented to us in everyday life.

Religious gratitude for all things is a loving response to the Creator's look of love. Our accepting the world with wonder and gratitude inspires our desire to treasure and care for the world. The possibility of our enjoying anything is based on a kind of humility that takes nothing for granted but lives in a continual state of surprise, recognizing all as gift, and—however implicitly—the Giver in the gift. Such gratitude and humility entail the appreciation of everything as the gift of Love Itself.

Pride, in contrast, is an attitude of entitlement, taking things for granted, and clamoring for more, in continual dissatisfaction; thus destroying everything, including happiness. The devastation of our landscapes and the decay of our townscapes—the ugliness of unloved persons, places, and things—often reflect the moral ugliness of our greed, indifference, and exploitation. Loveliness/beauty is rooted in Love Itself.

Our radical acceptance of and gratitude for everything and anything, which takes nothing for granted, makes happiness possible. Of course, such an attitude implies a religious foundation: our belief that all creation, including our own existence, is an un-

---

interior world of consciousness appropriating the exterior in its most particularized, individualized form. Inscape refers to the utter individuality and distinctiveness that marks each individual existence. . . . Instress refers to the fusion of the inscape of a given being with a given human consciousness in contact at a given moment with that being in all its uniqueness. Because the exterior universe can thus relate in its particular reality to human consciousness, to the self, the "I"—and not only to believing human selves, but to anyone with ordinary human sensitivity—the exterior universe can be related in Christian faith through the human self to God, who is "self-making" and who welcomes the exterior universe to himself through the human selves he has made.

[10]Karl Rahner, *Hearers of the Word* (London: Sheed & Ward, 1969) 106.

merited gift of Love Itself.[11] Our gratitude irradiates the splendor of the divine look of love that is the joy of our lives, making all things beautiful.[12]

[11] B. M. Kiely, *Psychology and Moral Theology* (Rome: Gregorian University Press, 1980) 228–30.

[12] The "Alternative Opening Prayer" for Sunday, 30 July 1995 (Seventeenth Sunday in Ordinary Time), synthesizes the key aspects of Beauty Itself at work in creation:

> God our Father,
> open our eyes to see your hand at work
> in the splendor of creation,
> in the beauty of human life.
> Touched by your hand our world is holy.
> Help us to cherish the gifts that surround
> us, to share your blessings with our
> brothers and sisters, and to experience
> the joy of life in your presence.
> We ask this through Christ our Lord. Amen.

2

In the Image and Likeness of Beauty Itself

Both Judaism and Christianity have affirmed that there is a basic and profound analogy between human existence and the very being of the living God. They have founded this affirmation on the words of Genesis (1:26-27): "And God said, 'Let us make man in our image and likeness.' So God created man in his own image; in the image of God he created him; male and female he created them." The doctrine of creation in the image of God expresses the biblical understanding of what it means to be human.[1]

What is the content of that image? The Bible speaks of four divine attributes that appeared to be communicable to creatures. These attributes could well represent analogies between God and the human image of God. When the psalmist, speaking in the name of God, admonished, "Do not behave like horse and mule, unreasoning creatures" (Ps 32:9), that appeared to assign to the human image the same rationality that was preeminently characteristic of the divine prototype. When the Sermon on the Mount urged, "There must be no limit to your goodness, as your heavenly Father's goodness knows no bounds" (Matt 5:48), that likewise ascribed to human life the capacity to mirror forth in some immanent but nevertheless distinct fashion the transcendent goodness of the heavenly Father. When the First Letter of John asserted that "God is love" and went on to urge that "he who dwells in

[1]Jaroslav Pelikan, *The Melody of Theology* (Cambridge, Mass.: Harvard University Press, 1988) 134.

love is dwelling in God'' (1 John 4:16), that, too, was a declaration that the ultimate mystery of the divine being had its counterpart in the human capacity to give love and to respond to love. And when the Gospels called God "Father," they were saying that human parenthood was patterned after its divine model. The concept of human personality, therefore, was part of the image of God, reflecting the personal quality of God to whom it was possible to pray as Father.

Much of this represents common ground between Judaism and Christianity, both of which affirm creation in the image of God on the basis of the first chapter of the Bible they have in common. But the Christian understanding of the concept has been distinctly and decisively affected by the community's faith that Jesus Christ, as Son of God and Son of Man, is the image of God in a unique, personal sense. Jesus Christ is not only the revelation of God to humankind, but the revelation of humankind to humankind—of humankind as God had intended humankind to be and as God planned for humankind to become again.

The content of the Christian doctrine of the "image of God" did not come only from the doctrine of the person of Christ. Taking off from the language of Genesis, "Let *us* make man in *our* own image," Augustine repeated the standard argument of most early Christian teachers that these plurals were proof of the doctrine of the Trinity in the very first narrative of the Bible. He suggested that the plurals were an indication that the "image of God" was itself Trinitarian. Therefore he devoted the second half of his *On the Trinity* to a review of possible Trinitarian vestiges in the human soul. Although these vestiges could not represent a perfect correspondence between Creator and creature, the triad of love, reason, and memory came close: each of these three was distinct from the other two, and yet together made one, single mind. That made the human mind an image of the Trinity: of the Father, who not only has love but "is love," according to 1 John 4:16; of the Son, who is reason or *logos,* according to the first verses of the Gospel of John (1:1-14); and, of the Holy Spirit, whose distinct function, according to the same Gospel, is to "call to mind all that I have told you" (14:26). These three were distinct "persons" and yet remained one single Godhead.[2]

[2]Ibid., 138.

The image of God metaphor implies that our knowledge of human nature and of God are correlated. Because humankind was originally in a right relationship with God, it was also in harmony with itself. It was what it was meant to be: human will and human reason were conformed to the divine will and the divine reason. The original righteousness of our first parents authentically imaged the divine will and reason to which it conformed. Original righteousness enabled us to image and imagine God rightly with a reliable human matrix for a true primal knowledge of God.

Just as humankind bore an analogy to the Creator, so the original temptation begins with an appeal to a false analogy (". . . you will be like God," Gen 3:5) and ends in the radical distortion of the true analogy. When the human mind and heart no longer conform to the divine mind will we fail to image and imagine/know God rightly? Our original likeness to God has become distorted by our own doing; consequently, our knowledge of God has become distorted. The pattern of human life in conformity to God's will/love is the image of God; self-will/idolatry in opposition to God disrupts that image. Truly good human lives are true images of God that reveal something of God's truth and goodness and beauty. Self-will is self-idolatry, the futile attempt to be our own little gods, yielding a distorted image of God. It is a futile attempt at self-glorification that withdraws us from our only true glory, the glory of God that our first parents reflected in their state of original righteousness as true images of God.

Christ, "the image of the invisible God" (Col 1:15), is the firstborn of a new creation. Unlike the first parents, who attempted to be their own little gods, Christ takes the form of God's servant (Phil 2:6-7), conforming his mind and will to God's mind and will.

The imagery of forming, shaping, and molding in the New Testament writing (e.g., 1 Cor 15; Phil 2:6-7) recalls the language of the original image passages in Genesis. This imagery found its way into the Christian tradition in the various terms deriving from the Latin root *form*. We speak of Christian formation, of the deformity of sin, of conformity to God's will and wisdom, of Jesus Christ's transformation of human life and of the reformation of Christian life.[3]

[3]John Navone, "The Image and Glory of God," *Homiletic and Pastoral Review* XC1/1 (October 1990) 65.

Christ, embodying in his own "form" the "image of the invisible God," forms our lives by enabling us through the gift of his Spirit to conform to his Father's will/love and wisdom. He reveals and accomplishes his Father's will for the transformation of all humankind, reminding us that his Father's will for us is always his Father's love for us. As the living and sacred image of God (Col 1:15-20; 2 Cor 3:12-18), Jesus Christ orients his community of faith to decision and action through the gift of his Spirit. If we cannot do what we cannot at least in some way imagine, Christ is the living image of God that enables us to imagine God as God truly is: absolutely credible, trustworthy, and lovable. As the true form/image of God, Jesus Christ enables our believing and hoping and loving. His words, "He who has seen me has seen the Father" (John 14:9), express the unique importance of his life as the definitive human image/form of God for knowing God and what it means to conform to God's will/love and wisdom/mind.

When Paul exhorts his readers to imitate him, assuring them that they have a model in him (Phil 3:17), he climaxes the account of his devotion to Christ with the hope that he may share in Christ's sufferings, becoming like him in his death (Phil 3:10). He uses the verb "to be conformed to" and "to take on the same shape as" *(symmorphizo)*. To be "in" Christ, for Paul, means to be transformed by Christ: "If anyone is in Christ, he is a new creation" (2 Cor 5:17). Just as God has molded shapeless clay into a human form in his original creation, so God re-creates or re-forms human persons "in Christ," his new creation. Paul asserts that the "new nature" that we have "put on" is being renewed in knowledge after the image of its creator (Col 3:10).

Paul's theology of human transformation appears in his Letter to the Romans (9:19-23) where God is portrayed as the potter or molder who shapes us like clay. He borrows the image from the Hebrew prophets (cf. Isa 29:16; 45:9; 64:8 and Jer 18:6) where it also relates back to the creation story of Adam (Gen 2). Paul expresses his new creation motif in terms of the plastic imagery of forming and molding.

Focusing specifically on the transformation process itself, the metamorphosis of grace, Paul affirms: "And we all, with unveiled face, beholding/reflecting the glory of the Lord, are being changed into his likeness from one degree of glory to another" (2 Cor 3:18). Paul employs the very same verb used for the *transfiguration* of

Jesus (Matt 17:2) and for that of Christians in the Letter to the Romans which exhorts them to "be *transformed* by the renewal of your mind" (12:2). Our new life/transfiguration implies that we share in the mind (truth) and love/will (goodness) and beauty (glory) of God as God's graced images. God is making us truthful, lovable/good and beautiful.

The Letter to the Hebrews opens with the announcement that God has now "spoken to us by a Son," who "reflects the glory of God and bears the very stamp *(charakter)* of his nature (1:2-3).[4] Metaphors of hearing, seeing and impressing a form describe Christian revelation in New Testament writings such as the story of Jesus' answer to the question about paying taxes, reported in the Synoptic Gospels (Mark 12:13-17 and parallels). Taking a coin, Jesus asks: "Whose likeness *(eikon)* and inscription is this?" Jesus, by assuming the coin to be one of the "things" of Caesar" because it bears Caesar's image, implies by analogy to "God's things," which are likewise to be rendered to God. Where God has impressed *God's* image, God's claim is to be recognized. God has stamped God's image in creation; God has stamped God's perfect image in God's new creation. God has given us God's perfect likeness in Jesus Christ. Through faith in him, we are conforming to God (Rom 12:2). God impresses God's image, embodied in Christ, on Christians who in turn express it in the true goodness and beauty of their words and deeds.

Christian worship, Scriptures, preaching, and deeds of justice and compassion express "God's things" or the impression that God is making on our minds and hearts and lives. God is revealed and self-communicates through the impression that God makes on all inspired to believe and to hope and to love through the gift

[4]The term *charakter* came from the impression on coins which was an exact impress, reduction, and representation of the original. The Fathers of the Church, in their defense of the First Council of Nicea, gave the word the status of a technical term of Christological and Trinitarian doctrine, which proved that the image and the one being imaged were identical, as the Nicene-Constantinopolitan Creed affirmed. See Jaroslav Pelikan, *Imago Dei: The Byzantine Apologia for Icons* (Princeton, N.J.: Princeton University Press, 1990) 176. The quality of being not merely an image, but an image by very nature, set the Son and Logos of God apart from all creatures and other images as well. For the Son of God was the one and only image of God that was the same as God in every respect.

of the Holy Spirit enabling us to follow Jesus, God's perfect image and true Word.

The life story of Jesus Christ is the beautiful icon disclosing God, Beauty Itself, to the world (John 12:45; 14:9). The crucified and risen Christ is the paradigmatic image for Christian faith of divine and human beauty. We are called to communicate the beauty of God by irradiating the Spirit of Jesus Christ in whom God is rendered visible, truly imaginable and credible as our way, our truth, and our life. Inasmuch as we cannot do what we cannot at least in some way imagine, Jesus Christ, the perfect image of Beauty Itself motivates our faith to accept his beautiful way of being-in-the-world as transfigured and transfiguring beings-with-others under the sovereignty of Supreme Beauty's love and wisdom. As the Son and Word of Beauty Itself incarnate, Jesus Christ makes God beautifully visible. He manifests the splendor of Supreme Beauty, the glory of the Father, that transfigures humankind into beautiful, living icons through the gift of the Spirit. Through the self-giving of the triune Beauty we become images of the transfigured and transfiguring Lord even in this present age (2 Cor 3:18) and much more so after the resurrection of the just (1 Cor 15:49; Rom 8:29).[5]

The perfect image of God, Jesus Christ, irradiates the transforming glory/beauty of God, the "splendor of his glory, the figure of his substance" (Heb 1:3). He is "the Lord of glory" (1 Cor 2:8), communicating the truth and goodness and beauty of God to humankind. The glory of God "on his face" (2 Cor 4:6) enables our vision of Supreme Beauty.[6] God's glory accompanied

[5]St. John of Damascus, in his *Homily on the Transfiguration of the Lord,* speaks of carrying in our hearts the beauty of the divine reality. He emphasizes that the Transfiguration was not an ontological change in the person of Christ, but a disclosure to the eyes of the disciples of what had been there all along. See Pelikan, *Imago Dei,* 92.

[6]Cyril of Alexandria (d. 444) asserted that the basis for all Christian eschatological hope was the resurrection of Jesus Christ; for humankind experienced, in Adam, the aversion of the face of God because of sin. But when the only-begotten Word of God became one of us and enriched us with his transforming Spirit, we were formed again and created anew. See Brian E. Daley, *The Hope of the Early Church* (Cambridge: Cambridge University Press, 1991) 110. Theodore of Mopsuestia (ca. 362–428) affirmed that our union with Christ, as a new race marked by faith and born anew in baptism,

his birth (Luke 2:9), baptism (Luke 4:21) and transfiguration (Luke 9:28-30; cf. 2 Pet 1:17-19). His illuminating goodness and truth and beauty both show the way to the Father and powerfully attract us to the Father. The illuminating beauty of Jesus Christ liberates us *from* the darkness that is alienation from Beauty Itself *for* the light that is communion with Beauty Itself.

The Fathers of the Church describe the central activity of heaven as communion with Beauty Itself. Augustine, especially in his 147th letter, the so-called *Book on Seeing God,* takes it as scripturally certain that the just shall see God.[7] Although the Scriptures affirm, in the words of 1 John 4:12 and 1 Timothy 6:16, that no one has ever seen God nor ever can see God, Augustine is able to distinguish between the eyes of the body, which cannot see a pure spirit, and the eyes of the spirit or the heart, which are capable of this. We shall see God in the communion of love that the redeemed will enjoy among themselves in the presence of God, Beauty Itself. The Fathers of the Church agree that no thing of beauty, no human loveliness enjoyed by the earthly eye, can do more than arouse nostalgia and longing for what is to be.[8] The most intense delight of the saints, illuminated by Beauty Itself, will be to see God.[9] In the light of Beauty Itself we shall see ourselves as we are seen: the image of God. We shall know ourselves as we are known: the brothers and sisters of Jesus Christ. We shall love ourselves as we are loved: the beloved sons and daughters of God.

The Greek Fathers interpreted the redemptive work of Jesus Christ in terms of his giving face to those without faces. The ancient Greeks called a slave a "no face," or "faceless one"

---

guarantees that his present state of glory, his life with God, will be communicated to us. See B. E. Daley, 114.

[7]Boniface Ramsely, *Beginning to Read the Fathers* (New York/Mahwah: Paulist Press, 1985) 226–27.

[8]Ibid., 228.

[9]J.N.D. Kelly, *Early Christian Doctrines,* 2nd ed. (New York: Harper and Brothers, 1960) 487. Kelly cites John Chrysostom about the most intense delight of the saints. He also refers to Cyril of Alexandria's understanding our redemption in Christ as the process of deification which attains its climax after the parousia and the resurrection, in which we shall contemplate "the beauty of the divine nature of our God and Father," 487.

(aposopos). When the Son of God assumed the features of a human face, God restored to us a face in God's own true image, chained as we have been like slaves without faces because of sin. Macarius the Great writes of the transforming and liberating beauty of the risen Christ:

> The soul which has been perfectly illuminated by that indescribable beauty of the luminous glory of the face of Christ and filled with the Holy Spirit . . . is all eye, all light, all face.[10]

The Greek Fathers' teaching on the sanctification or "divinization" *(theosis* or *theopoiesis)* implied what the transforming power of God, Beauty Itself, is doing for humankind. God is making humankind beautiful. The teaching of the Greek Fathers, dependent on 2 Peter 1:4 ("partakers of the divine nature"), designates that attainment to the likeness of God for which humankind was created in God's image (Col 3:10). It affirms that the transformation of believers from glory into glory has already begun (2 Cor 3:18).

The salvation that is the object of Christian hope involves the liberation of the whole creation from its bondage to decay/ugliness and the transfiguration of our bodies through resurrection, when all things participate in the glory/beauty of God (Rom 8:18-19; Phil 3:20-21). Paul awaits the ultimate triumph of God, Beauty Itself, in the saving and transfiguring power of Jesus Christ: "we await a Savior, the Lord Jesus Christ, who will change our lowly body to be like his glorious body, by the power which enables him to subject all things to himself" (Phil 3:20-21).

Corresponding to the classical triad of the Beautiful, the True, and the Good, though by no means identical with it, is the biblical triad of Jesus Christ as the Way, the Truth, and the Life (John 14:6). As Gregory of Nyssa put it, "He who said 'I am the Way' . . . shapes us anew in his own image," expressed, as Augustine said, in "the quality of beauty."[11] The Christian community affirms that Christ is the "true light that enlightens everyone" (John

[10]Homily 1, 2, PG 34, 451 AB, quoted in Michel Quenot, *The Icon* (London: Mowbray, 1992) 155.

[11]Gregory of Nyssa, *Against Eunomius* 2.10; Augustine, *On the Trinity* 6.10.11.

1:9), and the Life that is the source of all authentic goodness.[12] The same community believes that the beauty and glory proper to God who graciously communicates God's self to humankind as our ultimate fulfillment, may be seen fully with the eyes of faith only in the form of Jesus Christ. His Cross, no form of beauty for worldly eyes, reveals what God's beauty and glory are really about.[13] For those who see the Cross in the light of the resurrection, God's beauty appears as the glorious love which has extended its reign to include and transfigure what had been a kingdom of darkness and godlessness. The supreme beauty of Truth and Goodness Itself is seen in God's gracious love for God's creation. The crucified and risen Christ is the form and splendor of the Beautiful, the True, and the Good, which fulfills human desire and so brings humankind to communion with God.

Faith perceives the mystery of the divine love in its engagement with the world as revealed in Jesus Christ. It is in the form of this love that faith perceives its beauty, its uniqueness, and genuineness. The beautiful form of this love holds us captive, enabling us to see the pattern and shape of God's engagement with the world.[14] The Christian community is formed by the transform-

[12]Augustine, *Tractates on the Gospel of John* 22.8. See Jaroslav Pelikan, *Jesus Through the Centuries* (New York: Harper & Row, 1985) 7; Pelikan, *Fools for Christ: Essays on the True, the Good, and the Beautiful* (Philadelphia: Muhlenberg Press, 1955).

[13]The following section reflects the ideas of Hans Urs von Balthasar, *The Glory of the Lord: A Theological Aesthetics* (6 vols.), (San Francisco: Ignatius Press, 1982); H. U. von Balthasar, *Love Alone: The Way of Revelation* (London: Burns & Oates, 1968). In his opening volume of *The Glory of God,* von Balthasar traces the dialectic of subjective and objective evidence in revelation by showing how our perception of the form of the divine in the human is always intimately related to the transforming power of the content of that form upon us.

[14]Von Balthasar holds that in art, form strikes us as splendid because the delight it arouses is grounded on the deep truth and goodness of the reality which shows and offers itself there as something infinitely precious and fascinating. If we really perceive the form, we see it not just as a detached *Gestalt,* radiance, the glory of being. In contemplating the form we are "entranced" and "ravished" by this depth which appears in and through it. Von Balthasar recognizes that we have here a most useful analogy for the revelatory event. He cites the Nativity Preface in the Mass of the Roman Rite:

ing power of the glory that it beholds in the crucified and risen Christ. It knows the glory/beauty of divine love which captivates us in Christ, "the perfect image of God." The manifestation of that love on the cross grounds our conviction that despite appearances the world is grounded in love, in the boundless love which suffers all in order that it may draw all humankind to itself.

In Jesus Christ, the perfect image of God, Beauty Itself appears and grasps us in the very act of overwhelming us by his ineffable love.[15] Jesus Christ is the concrete form through which the splendor of God irradiates and transfigures humankind so

---

> By the Mystery of the Word made flesh
> the light of your glory has shown afresh
> upon the eyes of our mind, so that while
> we acknowledge him to be God seen by men
> we may be drawn by him to the love of things
> unseen.

God empowers the "eyes of the mind" with a new "light" so that we can recognize in a visual medium an object which is God's self, communicated through the sacramental mystery of the form of the Word Incarnate. In this vision there is, further, a "rapture" which carries us from the visible to the invisible reality made present in its sign, Jesus Christ. In speaking of the gift of faith we find ourselves offering an account of how we discover the form of the self-revealing God. But this discovery is never made without evoking a progressive transformation of the person who thereby receives the eyes to see the divine image pointing ever more clearly away from itself to the invisible God. In all sound aesthetics, according to von Balthasar, the doctrine of perception of the beautiful and the doctrine of ravishing power are ordered to each other. No one truly perceives without this self-transcending, ecstatic element of rapture. The phrase "the light of faith" presents an ambiguity: the glory of God in Christ can be seen only by the eyes of faith, but the eyes of faith can only see when the light of faith falls on them from the divine form of Jesus Christ. See *The Glory of God,* Vol. 1; and Aidan Nicholas, O.P., *The Art of God Incarnate* (London: Darton, Longman and Todd, 1980) 137.

[15]When theologians speak of humankind made in the image of God, or of the world as a created thing, they are not speaking about something which they see and know for themselves. Instead they are relying on a divine communication which can in no way be inferred or deduced from the empirical reality of the world and of humankind. In short, there is no theology if there is no such thing as revelation. Theology is the attempt to interpret the documents of divine revelation preserved by sacred tradition.

that, through the gift of his Spirit, we become one spirit with God, beautiful in Beauty Itself, good in Goodness Itself. The image of Beauty Itself in Jesus Christ draws us out of ourselves into the realm of Beauty Itself; for Jesus Christ is the glory of God liberating us from our futile attempts at self-glorification.[16] The splendor of God, Beauty Itself, in Jesus Christ transports us into the realm of God's delight/joy.

> Something which has existed since the beginning
> that we have heard,
> and we have seen with our own eyes;
> that we have watched
> and touched with our hands:
> the Word, who is life—
> this is our subject.
> That life was made visible:
> we saw it and we are giving our testimony,
> telling you of the eternal life
> which was with the Father
> and has been made visible to us.
> What we have seen and heard
> we are telling you
> so that you too may be in union with us,
> as we are in union with the Father,
> and with his Son Jesus Christ.
> We are writing this to you to make our joy complete.
>
> 1 John 1:1-4

[16]See *The Weekly Missal* (London: Collins, 1982) for references to the image-of-God theme in Prefaces to the Mass.

Preface of Epiphany (p. 1340):

> "Today you revealed in Christ your eternal plan of salvation and showed him as the light of all peoples. Now that his glory has shone among us you have renewed humanity in his immortal image."

Preface of Lent I (p. 1341):

> "As we recall the great events that gave us new life in Christ, you bring the image of your Son to perfection within us."

Weekday Preface III (p. 1347):

> "Through your beloved Son you created our human family. Through him you restored us to your likeness."

Preface of Sundays V (p. 67 of *The Sunday Missal*, London: Collins):

> "All things are of your making, all times and seasons obey your laws, but you chose to create man in your own image, setting him over the whole world in all its wonder."

The Cross of Jesus reveals the glory of God as the mystery of Trinitarian self-giving love in solidarity with all humankind: God sharing God's own life and freedom. The Cross and resurrection reveal the glory/beauty of an invincible love which all the powers of evil, even death itself, cannot quench. The beauty of God's love is our joy/delight forever (John 14:27; 16:33).

Some Prefaces explicitly refer to beauty:

The Dedication of a Church II (p. 1353, *The Weekly Missal):*

> "You give us grace upon grace to build the temple of your spirit, creating its beauty from the holiness of our lives."

Preface of the Immaculate Conception (p. 1355):

> "Full of grace, she was to be a worthy mother of your Son, your sign of favor to the Church at its beginning, and the promise of its perfection as the bride of Christ, radiant in beauty."

Preface of All Saints (p. 1361) implies the beauty/glory and joy link:

> "Their glory fills us with joy, and their communion with us in your Church gives inspiration and strength as we hasten on our pilgrimage of faith, eager to meet them."

Preface of Marriage III (p. 1362) sees divine love reflected in human love:

> "You created man in love to share your divine love. We see his high destiny in the love of husband and wife, which bears the imprint of your own divine love. . . . The love of man and woman is made holy in the sacrament of marriage, and becomes the mirror of your everlasting love."

3

The Power of Beauty

Beauty has the subtle power of attracting or calling us. The Greeks recognized this when they named the beautiful *to kalon,* from the verb *kaleo,* meaning to call or beckon.[1] True beauty is the attractiveness of whatever is truly good for us. Inasmuch as human achievement entails the attractiveness of particular goods, beauty is a precondition for all concrete human achievements.

Beauty, in fact, is at the heart of all human motivation, decision, and action; for we do not decide and act unless we are moved by the attractiveness of a particular good. Every vocation is a response to the attractiveness of a good that calls or beckons us. True beauty is the motivating attractiveness of a good that draws us to adherence, commitment, and genuine achievement. Life without beauty would be unmotivated, mere drift, and less than truly human.

The Meaning of Beauty

True beauty as attractiveness of the truly good motivates human life and development in that intellectual, moral, and religious self-transcendence that constitutes human authenticity.[2] Without their attractiveness of beauty, intellectual, moral, and religious goods

[1]Armand E. Maurer, C.S.B., *About Beauty* (Houston: Center for Thomistic Studies, University of St. Thomas, 1983) 105.

[2]Bernard Lonergan, S.J., *Method of Theology* (London: Darton, Longman and Todd, 1972) 104.

are bereft of their power to transform human life. Beauty is the enabling power of the truly good to draw us out of ourselves for the achievement of excellence. The macho bias which tends to disregard beauty as superfluous, ornamental, and "feminine," overlooks the indispensable power of beauty for the attainment of human happiness and fulfillment.

We cannot live without beauty. Our need for beauty is felt in the most basic demands of the human mind and heart, which Lonergan identifies as the five transcendental precepts: Be attentive, be intelligent, be reasonable, be responsible, be in love.[3] Beauty is the power of the good to command, to focus, and to sustain the attention necessary for our becoming intelligent, reasonable, responsible, and loving. It is the power to motivate and sustain inquiry and understanding, reflection and judgment, deliberation, evaluation, decision, and action. The attractiveness of human achievement and excellence inspires admiration or marveling esteem accompanied by gratification and joy.

True love, friendship, commitment, and community are related to beauty.[4] Plato and the philosophies derived from him maintain that beauty is the quality that makes someone or something the object of possible love. Augustine affirms, "Only the beautiful is loved . . . we cannot help loving what is beautiful."[5] If this is true, and if the old definition is right—*pulchrum est quod visu placet,* to be beautiful means to be "pleasing to see"—then there can be no true love without approving contemplation.

The creative power of Beauty Itself is reflected in the procreative power of human beauty and sexual attraction. The reciprocal attractiveness of beauty of male and female is the starting point for most human life stories. Human existence itself evidences the life-giving power of divine and human beauty. To be or not to be is the question of beauty and its motivating power.

[3]Ibid., 270.

[4]John Navone, *Self-giving and Sharing: The Trinity and Human Fulfillment* (Collegeville, Minn.: The Liturgical Press, 1989) 136–37. Chapters ten and eleven treat of beauty: "The Church: Icon of the Trinity," and "Communion in Beauty and Beauty in Communion."

[5]*Confessions* 14, 3; *On Music (De Musica)* 6, 13. The german word *schön* (beautiful) is linked with *schauen* (to see); its literal meaning is "worth seeing."

Beauty According to the Theologians

Aquinas, in his commentary on the *Divine Names* of Pseudó-Dionysius, claims that divine beauty is the motive of creation.[6] Because God loves the divine beauty, God wishes to share it as much as possible by communicating this likeness to creatures. God is the cause of their radiance. Each form imparted to a creature is a beautifying participation in the divine radiance; and since being *(esse)* comes from form, Aquinas affirms that beauty is the course of the existence of all things.[7] Out of love for divine beauty God gives existence to everything, and moves and conserves everything. God has created the universe to make it beautiful for God's self by reflecting this same beauty. God, Beauty Itself, intends everything to become beautiful in the fullness of the divine beauty.

Aquinas considers beauty to be among the essential names of God, describing God's very nature. He finds a special reason for ascribing beauty to the Son, to the image of the Father; for we especially associate beauty with images. The Son is the perfect likeness of the Father, because he perfectly shares the Father's divine nature. He is the Father's Word, radiant and clear. When we speak, the light of our minds shines forth in our words and gives them clarity. Our words are clear to the extent that our thinking is clear. When God the Father utters the divine Word, it completely expresses God and all the intelligible clarity of God's mind.[8]

The divine beauty took visible form when the Word of God was made flesh and lived among us.[9] Christ has the divine beauty, for he shares the divine nature. As Paul affirms: "He was in the form of God" (Phil 2:6) and "In Christ the fullness of deity resides in bodily form" (Col 2:9). Secondly, Aquinas continues, Christ had the beauty of the moral virtues, especially justice and truth. He was "full of grace and truth" (John 1:14). Christ had

[6]*In Div. Nom.* c. 4, lect. 5, n. 349.

[7]Ibid., n. 349. Divine beauty causes the harmony and order of the whole universe. Beauty wields a power over things, giving them whatever unity they have: among rational creatures, their agreement in ideas, and their love and friendship.

[8]ST I, q. 39, a. 8; *In 1 Sent.,* d. 31, a. 1.

[9]*In Psalmos* 44:2; ed. Vivès, Vol. XVIII, 503–5.

the loveliness of upright and virtuous moral behavior. Through grace (the very word is redolent of beauty) we know the beauty of God; we delight in seeing God's perfect image and in hearing the incarnate Word.[10]

The theology of beauty entails definite presuppositions. God is where God acts. God acts wherever anything exists. God acts in originating, sustaining, and bringing to perfection all that is good and true and beautiful. God is known in divine activity as Creator, Sustainer, Perfecter, and Fulfillment of all that is knowable (true), lovable (good), and delightful (beautiful). Nothing exists apart from God, the Origin and Ground and Destiny of all that is. Nothing is knowable, lovable, or delightful independent of God, the ultimate context/meaning of all that is true and good and beautiful. Nothing is truly knowable, lovable, and delightful out of context. God is Supreme Truth, Goodness, and Beauty, the norm and measure of all dependent or participated truth and goodness and beauty.

God acts consciously knowing divine truth, consciously loving divine goodness, and consciously enjoying/delighting in divine beauty. God's knowing and loving and enjoying creatures is not a response to them; rather, they exist because God knows and loves and delights in the divine self. (Our artistic activity offers analogy. We, too, create by our interior seeing; our painting is its expression. We do not merely see and record a scene of beauty; we create it. What we have seen is enriched by our seeing; it comes into its own in our vision of it.) Nothing is knowable (true) or lovable (good) or delightful (beautiful) apart from God's consciously knowing and loving and delighting in the divine self. Our finite knowledge and love and delight are, ultimately, rooted in God's knowing and loving and delighting.[11] God's knowing and

[10]Through the light of glory, the saints in heaven will see the beauty of God clearly, and be ravished by it. See ST I, q. 12, a. 2c. This fulfills Christ's promise: "Then the saints will shine like the sun in their Father's kingdom" (Matt 13:43).

[11]Human suffering, loving, and delighting are activities which Aquinas contextualizes in God: "God is the cause of all action insofar as he grants the power of acting, which he preserves and brings into act, and insofar as it is through his power that every other power is active. When we realize that God is his own power and that he dwells in every being, not as part of its essence but as holding it in being, it follows that God himself must act di-

loving and delighting are implicitly expressed in all that makes knowable, lovable, and delightful. God is the Common Good of all creation: all created goodness participates in and depends on God's goodness.[12]

Supreme Being Incarnate

Mark's account of the baptism (1:11) and the transfiguration (9:7) of Jesus, in which the voice from heaven affirms Jesus as the Beloved Son, implies that he is equally the Beautiful Son in whom the Father is eternally delighted and pleased. God lovingly contemplates and affirms the divine beauty: "You are my beloved Son; my favor rests on you" (1:11). The baptism of Jesus is a theophany, a manifestation of God's truth, goodness, and beauty. Similarly, the transfiguration of Jesus reveals the divine glory that will transfigure all humankind. Beauty Itself manifests itself and beckons, calls/attracts us to itself in Jesus Christ, to the transfiguration that awaits all humankind.[13]

---

rectly in every agent; this, however, does not exclude the action of the will and of nature" (*Questiones disputatae de potentia Dei,* 3, 7). Again Aquinas asserts that "Since God is the universal cause of all being, it is thus necessary that wherever being is found, God is also there present" (*Summa contra Gentiles,* 3, 68).

[12]No created good is a common good in an absolute sense, because it cannot be the final cause of all reality. There is a hierarchy of created goods reflecting, in varying degrees, the universal actuality of God who is the transcendent Common Good towards which all common goods of the universe are oriented and from which they receive their character of the common good (ST I, q. 60, a. 5).

[13]Michel Quenot affirms that the Transfiguration is the keystone of Byzantine doctrines concerning the vision of God: "The icon is indeed a vision of God made man and of His deifying grace manifested in men. It is the prototype and not just the portrait of our future *transfigured* humanity; it expresses the new order of the cosmos, where beasts and mankind live together in harmony. . . . At our creation, the image of God was deeply engraved in us, but it was defaced by the Fall of our first parents. It is restored to us again by our participation in the Incarnation of Christ, and above all by our Baptism. Yet our resemblance to God results from our acquiring the Holy Spirit, which is realized according to each person's capacity (1 Cor 15:41-43)." M. Quenot's *The Icon* (London: Mowbray, 1992) 153.

Jesus Christ manifests and communicates God's knowing his truth, loving his goodness, and delighting in his beauty. John's Gospel underscores the joy/delight of Jesus Christ. It is the fullness of joy (3:29) that Jesus desires to share with his disciples (15:11); it will transform their sorrow into joy (16:20). Jesus associates with the joy of a new birth, a new life (16:21). He promises the fullness of joy that no one can take from us (16:22); that his Father will give it to those who ask for anything in Jesus' name (16:24). Jesus Christ is God's Word of truth (e.g., 1:14; 17:17) in whom we recognize that "God is love" (1 John 4:8, 16) and communicates the fullness of God's joy/delight. John affirms that in Jesus Christ "The Word was made flesh, he lived among us, and we saw his glory, the glory that is his as the only Son of the Father, full of grace and truth" (1:14). Beauty Itself manifests and communicates itself to all humankind in the glory and grace and truth and joy/delight that is the only Son of the Father. The Father has given us the Son and Spirit that we might share the triune God's eternal happiness in a life of truth and goodness and beauty.

The beauty of the Father draws us to the Son (John 6:44); for seeing Jesus is to see the Father (John 14:9). Seeing the supreme beauty of the Father in God's only Son brings joy and gladness. Abraham rejoiced and was glad to see Jesus' day (John 8:56). We have seen the glory of the only Son (John 1:14), the perfect image of the invisible God (Col 1:15), the "splendor" of God's glory (Heb 1:3), who will draw all persons to himself when he is lifted up (John 12:32). The crucified and glorified Jesus irradiates the supreme beauty of the one and true God whose love draws all to himself, that God's joy might become ours and ours might become complete (John 15:11). Beauty Itself, as Paul implies, will gradually free us from all that obscures it: "My children for whom I suffer the pain of giving birth until Christ is formed in you" (Gal 4:19). Beauty Itself transfigures the world in the self-giving love of the crucified and glorified Christ.

The "glory" of God is known wherever the truth and goodness and beauty of God attract, beckon, transform, and delight us. God's beauty irradiates God's truth and goodness, and draws all creation to itself. To know God, in the biblical sense, is to delight in God. Our communion as friends of God with a knowing and loving and delighting God means our sharing in God's knowing and loving and delighting; it means our sharing in God's truth and goodness and beauty. If seeing Jesus is to see the Father, seeing the friends of God is to see God, even if in a glass darkly. One must welcome the Light which is God's self (John 1:9; 8:12), so that we may see with purified eyes what God sees: the splendor of divine love which transfigured the world. Such beauty eludes the purely aesthetic because it requires an interior light for whoever contemplates it. The wondrous splendor of divine beauty is perceived only by persons in communion with Beauty Itself, the pure of heart who see God in all things.

What Jesus promises his followers in the Beatitudes is the joy of communion with God. The pure of heart shall delight in seeing God (Matt 5:8); and ". . . we shall be like him, for we shall see him as he is" (1 John 3:2). Aquinas detected in the sequence of the Beatitudes a progress in joy from the recognition of our need for God, to participation in God's reconciling love.[14] The fellowship of joy is that of the crucified and risen Christ. The Beatitudes express the joy of the way of the Cross in loving God above all, the joy of the poor who have God alone for support (Pss 1, 34, 40, 84, 112, etc.). Although the fullness of joy belongs to the final consummation in the beatific vision of Beauty Itself, it is even now known in a partial and inchoate way (1 Cor 13:12). Such joy evidences our seeing the beauty of God's true goodness in our lives.

God, who alone is good (Mark 10:18), is the source and foundation of true glory or beauty (Ps 62:6, 8). When Satan attempts to seduce Jesus with "all the kingdoms of the world and their glory," Jesus answers: "The Lord your God shall you adore and him only shall you worship" (Matt 4:8-10). Seductive beauty, as opposed to true beauty, is the attractiveness or allure of the apparent good that would undermine human excellence and its concomitant joy and gladness.[15] Excellence, divine and human,

[14]ST II-I, q. 69.

[15]Aquinas asserts (ST I-II, q. 78, a. 1, ad 2) that we do not strive after evil for its own sake; that we will nothing unless it is good, either real or apparent (*Contra Gentiles* 4, 92); that we do not strive towards evil by tending towards anything but by turning away from something. Just as a thing is called good by reason of its participation in goodness, so a thing is called evil by reason of its turning away from good (*Questiones disputatae de poten-*

irradiates true beauty and evokes joy/delight. Persons who are what God is calling them to be reflect the beauty and communicate the joy/delight of the God they seek and serve. Hence, to see Jesus is to see the beauty and know the joy of the Father for whom he lives.

The desert monks of ancient Christendom associated devils and demons with seductive beauty.[16] They describe devils as beguiling, tempting creatures, representing all the enticements of the world and its beauty, but also as monstrous beings who frighten and attack the monk. The temptations of the Fathers of the desert alternate between two representatives of diabolical power: seductive beauty and horrid ugliness.

In one case, the Seducer is presented in human or suprahuman form: as a person of astounding beauty or an angel of light. Early Greek Christians depict the devil as a handsome, charming young man or woman. They recognized that evil can be so powerfully attractive and seductive that we cede or consent to its temptation. The appropriate symbol for the Seducer/Tempter had to be personal and appealing; it has to be apparently good.

The art of the Middle Ages preferred to portray the devil as an ugly and horrifying monster. It stressed the effects rather than the cause of our succumbing to temptation. The horrifying subhuman shape, part human, part animal, symbolized how personal evil alters and deforms our natural corporeal and spiritual integrity. A deformed, quasi-bestial, and less-than-human figure represented the effects of our turning away from the true beauty/glory which God alone can give.

---

tia Dei 3, 6, 14); that nothing is so very evil that it cannot have some appearance of good; and by reason of such goodness it is able to move desire (*Questiones disputatae de veritate* 22, 6, 6); that "If evil were taken away from some part of the universe, then much of its perfection would disappear, for its beauty arises from the orderly union of good and evil, while evil springs from the waning away of good. Nevertheless, by the foresight of the governor of the universe, good follows from evil just as the song receives its sweetness from the interval of silence" (*Contra Gentiles* 3, 71).

[16]John Navone, *Triumph Through Failure* (Homebush, Australia: St. Paul Publications, 1984) 72–73. See John Navone, "Satan Returns," in *The Furrow* 26 (no. 9, September 1975) 541–50.

John's Gospel tells of four loves that lead us away from the glory/beauty of God.[17] We resist and reject God because we love the darkness (3:19); we love human approval (12:43); we love our own lives (12:25); and we love the world (1 John 2:15). The first three are disordered self-love, love of self independently of God; the fourth means the love of the forces that resist and oppose God's self-giving.

Jesus is the light of the world (8:12; 9:5). Refusal to accept the light is motivated by the love of darkness, of the absence of the light which is Christ, of the world without God (whose manifestation is in Christ) that is in the darkness. With Christ's coming, "the light shines in the darkness" (1:5). Because we are free to leave the darkness and come to the light (12:35), our refusal represents a decision to remain in the state without Christ and therefore without God. Remaining in the darkness corresponds to remaining willfully in the state of persons without God (12:46). Walking in the darkness means living and acting in the state of separation from God (8:12; 12:35; 1 John 1:6). Darkness is the state of human consciousness which results from our attachment to works done in opposition to God.

John believes that a person loves what is "his or her own." Were the apostles "of the world," the world would certainly cherish them because they would be "its own" (15:19). Christians also love what is their own (1 John 3:7-15). Evil persons love the darkness, the state of their own making; they love what they have, or are apart from and without God. Their attachment to what they have independently of God closes their minds and hearts to the life and love which God offers them in Christ.

Those who seek self-advancement or self-exaltation (7:8; 8:50) cannot adhere in faith to Jesus because they are primarily concerned about the attainment of their glory and human approval; they have abdicated all desire for the authentic approval which comes from God alone; they prefer the honor given them independently of God. Such greatness is illusory and false because it is of human making apart from God, the source of all true greatness. Love of what we hold independently of God prevents our welcoming of God's self-giving in Christ.

[17] John Navone, "Divine and Human Conflict," *Priests and People* (March 1990) 94.

There is a self-love which values what we are and have in this world above Christ himself and leads to the loss of eternal life/love. Christ condemns the love of self in preference to himself (12:25).

The longing of the flesh, the longing of the eyes, and the haughty airs of this life constitute the love of the world that cannot come from the Father. The first two (1 John 2:16) are a craving for self-satisfaction; the third is self-exaltation. Such loves are irreconcilable with the love that derives from the Father; they represent love for a godless state of self-seeking without God.

John associates four loves with Christian faith: love for the glory of God (12:43), love for the light (3:19), love for Christ (8:42-47), and the love of God (5:40; 1 John 2:15). These are aspects of the Father's love that we welcome through God's glorified Son. We are not left orphans; for through Jesus Christ we now know who God is and that God loves us. An orphan does not know or is deprived of the source of his or her being; however, through Jesus we recognize and love our Father, the source of our lives. Whoever loves Jesus Christ loves the Father. Those who love God's glory manifested in Jesus have the love of God within them and are becoming transformed by it; whereas those who love themselves above all, who desire a glory and approval independent of the true glory that they can enjoy from God in Jesus Christ or who love the evil which they have apart from God, can only reject the Father's love and refuse to believe. In Jesus Christ the external manifestation of God's inner being and therefore of our inalienable destiny, here and hereafter, has reached its climax. It is by faith and acceptance of this challenge that we enter the new creation and begin to return toward our divinely given destiny in love for God above all and sharing God's universal love for others. Jesus is the ultimate manifestation of the God who is love, revealing to the world the inner life of God's dynamic interpersonal love and in that revelation showing also what the human community of earth must become when transfigured by Beauty Itself.

The Witness of the Saints and Scripture

Among the saints witnessing to the beauty of God is Augustine who, after recalling his wayward life, exclaimed: "Late have I loved you, O Beauty ever ancient, ever new, late have I loved you."[18] Angela of Foligno (1248–1309) recounts a vision of God: "There I beheld a beauty so great that I can say nothing concerning it, save that I saw supreme Beauty, containing within itself all goodness."[19] John of the Cross (1542–91) tells of his religious experience of divine beauty: ". . . all the beauty of creatures, compared with the infinite beauty of God, is the height of deformity."[20]

The Book of Wisdom describes God as the source of beauty in the world. It condemns pagans for worshipping the sun, moon, and stars as gods because of their beauty, reminding them that the true God, creator of all beauty, far surpasses them (13:3-5). Wisdom literature also affirms that the words of wisdom are beautiful (Prov 1:9; 4:9). The psalmist describes God as "clothed with beauty," as having "put on praise and beauty," as having "praise and beauty . . . before him" (Pss 92:1; 103:1; 95:6).

The eschatological passages of the Old Testament abound in references to what is beautiful.[21] There is mention of the future beauty of Jerusalem (Isa 52:1; 62:3; Zech 9:17), and of the Messiah (Isa 33:17). At the end God as such will become a beautiful diadem for God's people (Isa 28:5). Isaiah foretells the joy of Israel in the last days when it "shall see the glory of the Lord, and the beauty of our God" (35:2). The beauty of God inspires eschatological joy and delight.

Glory and beauty are central to the thought of Paul.[22] In the beginning we were subject to God and could see divine glory and enjoy divine beauty (Rom 1:21, 23). As soon as we became subject to sin we no longer saw God's glory or enjoyed divine beauty (Rom 3:23; 2 Thess 1:9). After the death and resurrection of Jesus Christ, we were liberated from the domination of sin, and we see the glory and enjoy the beauty of God in the face of Christ (2

[18]*Confessions* IX, 10.

[19]*The Divine Consolation of Blessed Angela of Foligno* in *Anthology of Mysticism,* ed. P. de Jaegher (Westminster, Md.: New Press, 1950) 28.

[20]Ibid., 145–46.

[21]G. Henton Davies, "Beauty," *The Interpreter's Dictionary of the Bible,* ed. G. A. Buttrick (New York/Nashville: Abingdon Press, 1962) 1:372.

[22]M. Carrez, "Glory," J. J. Von Allman, *Vocabulary of the Bible* (London: Lutterworth Press, 1961, 4th impression) 141.

Cor 3:18; 4:6). With the final return of Christ, we will neither sin nor die anymore; not only will we see the glory and enjoy the beauty of God, but we ourselves will become glorious and beautiful (1 Cor 15:3; 2 Cor 3:18; Phil 3:21), fully receptive to the radiant splendor of the Lord.

Outside Pauline literature and John's Gospel the notion of glory or beauty may be understood in three ways: (1) the active and radiant presence of God helping God's people (Luke 2:9; 9:31; Rev 18:1); (2) the glory or beauty wherever God rules or reigns: the Temple (Rev 15:8); the New Jerusalem (Rev 21:10); (3) as a characteristic of the Messianic Age or heaven (Mark 8:38; 13:26; 10:37; Matt 25:31-46).

The glory or beauty of God is affirmed wherever the divine supreme goodness is manifested in helping God's people. In the present world we may already perceive endlessly diverse manifestations of God's radiant goodness towards us; in the world to come we shall behold it in its fullness and reflect its beauty. The vision of God as God is, will be the eternal delight of all who have been gloriously transfigured by the splendor of divine love.

The Beauty of the Good Shepherd Draws All to Himself

When John's Gospel affirms that Jesus is "the Good Shepherd" (John 10:11), the original Greek adjective used to qualify shepherd is *kalos.* As applied to both things and persons, the epithet may be translated as "organically healthy," "fit," "useful," "serviceable." It also means "beautiful in respect to sensual impression," in the sense of "pleasant," "attractive," "lovely." Finally, it may describe the inward disposition of a person. Here it means "morally good." The Greek, in speaking of *kalos,* understood the total state of soundness, health, wholeness, and order, whether in external appearance or internal disposition.[23]

In his commentary on Jesus as the Good Shepherd, Brown tries to capture the idea of *kalos* as "attractive," "beauty-as-it-shows-

[23]W. Grundmann, *"Kalos," Theological Dictionary of the New Testament,* ed. G. Kittel (Grand Rapids, Mich.: Wm. B. Eerdmans, 1964–76) 10:536–37.

itself in outward form."[24] Christ not only fulfills the idea of the authentic shepherd, but he also fulfills the idea of the true shepherd's attractive loveliness. Brown, therefore, translates the word *kalos* not by "good," but by "model" or "noble." He believes that the Greek *kalos* means "beautiful" in the sense of an ideal or model of perfection. The epithet implies the correspondence between the nobility of the conception and the beauty of the realization. The "good" is not only good inwardly *(agathos),* but good as perceived *(kalos).* Jesus, in the fulfillment of his work as "the Good Shepherd," claims the admiration of all that is generous in us.[25] This implies the intimate relationship between the shepherd and the sheep. The goodness/beauty of the shepherd cannot be understood without reference to the sheep. Jesus as the Good Shepherd is "good"/"beautiful" in such a way as to draw all persons to himself (John 12:32). And the beauty of his goodness, which saves the world, is supremely seen in the act by which he would so draw them, wherein he lays down his life for the sheep.[26] This good which is perceived finds its concretization in the saving work of Jesus. John uses the adjective *kalos* four other times in his Gospel: twice in 2:10 in reference to the water that Jesus changed into wine at the wedding of Cana and twice in 10:32-33 in reference to the works of Jesus. The Word, in John's Gospel, is applied uniquely to Jesus or to his mission. It affirms the excellence and uniqueness of Jesus as the shepherd of the new people of God, fulfilling in himself and going beyond all the former Old Testament prototypes as their messianic fulfillment.[27] He came "not to condemn the world, but that the world might be saved through him" (John 3:17). He came "that they may have life, and have it abundantly" (John 10:10), by laying down his life for his sheep.

[24]R. Brown, *The Gospel According to John,* Vol. II (Garden City, New York: Doubleday and Co., 1966–70) 386.

[25]B. F. Westcott, *The Gospel According to St. John* (Grand Rapids, Mich.: Eerdmans, repr. 1981) 154.

[26]W. Temple, *Readings in St. John's Gospel* (London: Macmillan, 1950) 166.

[27]I. De La Potterie, "Le Bon Pasteur" in *Populus Dei: Studi in onore del Card. Alfredo Ottaviani per il cinquantesimo di sacerdozio: 18 marzo 1966,* 2 vols. (Rome: Communio 10–11, 1969) 952.

4

Beauty: God's Delight

If God knows divine truth, loves divine goodness, and delights in divine beauty, a theology of beauty will have to concern the delight and joy and happiness of God. Aquinas affirms that in God alone is it true that God's very being is God's being happy.[1] Whatever God is, is God's happiness; this is not something extrinsic to God, but the very life or eternal activity of God. The triune God eternally delights in the beauty of its true goodness.

If the beautiful, as Aquinas asserts, is "that which when seen gives pleasure," the "seeing" and "pleasure" of God's delight in divine beauty are not physical; for "God is spirit" (John 4:24).[2] Both the divine and human "seeing" and "pleasure" of God's delight in beauty are spiritual; both entail the cognitive and affective consciousness of knowing and loving subjects. Beauty Itself, the origin and ground and perfection of all created beauty, is Spirit; and the transcendent Spirit of God is equally supreme goodness and truth. The *good* and *true* and *being,* Aquinas af-

[1]Aquinas, *Summa Theologiae,* I-II, q. 3, a. 2. "Perfect beatitude belongs naturally to God alone, as in him being and beatitude are identical. For the creature, however, beatitude is not a natural possession but its last end" (ST I, q. 62, a. 4).

[2]ST II-II, q. 152, a. 4, ad 3. Some observations of Aquinas regarding delight/enjoyment: It is good in the highest degree because it is perfect rest in a sublime good (ST II-II, q. 34, a. 3, ad 2); it arises from a real union with good (*Summa contra Gentiles,* 1, 90); it arises from love for something/one (ST I-II, q. 31, a. 6).

firms, are one and the same reality, but in the mind they are distinguished from each other."[3]

God sees all that God has made, and it is very good. It is good because God sees it, because God sees it as good. God's vision is not a response to created beauty; it is its cause.[4] God's cognitive and affective delight in divine beauty creates, sustains, and brings to perfection all created beauty. God's vision of and delight in divine beauty is the ultimate context, measure, and fulfillment of all created beauty. Inasmuch as God is the giver of all created beauty, it is the manifestation of divine grace and is measured by the demands of the divine intention for our ultimate fulfillment, union with God, in the beatific vision of God as such, sharing God's vision of and delight in God's beauty.[5]

God's gift of the Spirit enables us to share, even now in a glass darkly, God's vision of and delight in divine beauty. The Spirit is given to us to be a source of living water, welling up from our hearts (John 7:38). God works within us, within our hearts and minds, within our freedom.[6] God's gift of the Spirit is that power of divine life, of light, of goodness, of truth and beauty, welling up within us and almost compelling us to surrender ourselves to it, to become its vehicle of expression. From it that new life proceeds, and that means that anything that is not a true expression of us will not be an expression of God either. The converse, in some sense, is also true. What is not an expression of God will not be a true expression of us.[7] We are made to reflect the image

[3]ST I-II, q. 29, a. 5.

[4]Simon Tugwell, O.P., *Reflections on the Beatitudes* (London: Darton Longman & Todd Ltd., 1980) 109.

[5]John Navone and Thomas Cooper, *Tellers of the Word* (formerly Le Jacq; now published [1981] by Jesuit Educational Center for Human Development, Cambridge, Mass., 105). Aquinas affirms that the ultimate happiness and beatitude of any intellectual being is to know God (*Summa contra Gentiles,* 3, 25). Since the soul is created directly by God, it will not be completely happy unless it sees God directly (*Quaestiones quodlibetales* 10, 17). Since the enjoyment of God, deservedly, due to his excellence, surpasses the power of all creatures, it follows that his complete and perfect joy does not enter into us but rather we enter into it. "Enter into the joy of your Lord" (Matt 25:21) (ST II-II, q. 28, a. 3).

[6]Aquinas, *Commentary on the Gospel of St. Matthew,* 849.

[7]Simon Tugwell, O.P., *Reflections on the Beatitudes,* 96.

and likeness of God, and it is that image and likeness which is restored by grace, by the working of the Holy Spirit. Our purity of heart is not just a matter of our interiority. Jesus tells his disciples that they are pure because of the word that he has spoken to them (John 15:3). If we have the purity of heart that shares God's vision and delight it is because God has given us a pure heart. The water welling up unto everlasting life proceeds from the Father and the Son. It is God dwelling in us who gives us a true interiority that is genuinely ours, but not simply our own.[8] Within my own interiority in myself is God's interiority in me; and, as Augustine affirms, God is even more intimately within me than I am in myself.[9] There is really only one source of life in us, and that is fully human only in being also divine. God is the heart of our heart; so, our created freedom can really subsist as such only if it is rooted in God's freedom.[10] The essential source of my identity is God, the mystery at the source of myself. Because the mystery of God and the mystery of my soul belong together, God's vision and delight affect me. If our life is rooted in God, so that the wellspring of life in us is God, then we shall see and delight as God sees and delights. And what God sees and delights in is God. This is why the pure of heart will see God. In one sense, God does not see anything but God. God does not have two different kinds of vision, one for seeing God's own self and another for seeing creatures.[11] God sees all that God has made within the eternal and delightful contemplation of the divine self.[12] That is why God sees that it is very good.

To enjoy the beatitude of the pure heart means that wherever you look, whatever you are looking at, what you see is God. God, revealing God's self in myriads of different ways, but always God. It means having a source of life welling up from the eternity of God that enables you to look at the crucified Christ and know that you are seeing God. It means recognizing a mystery within

[8]St. Irenaeus, *Against the Heresies* V 9:1.

[9]Augustine, *Confessions* III, 11.

[10]Part of human dignity is that we are the source of our own actions, just as God is the source of God's own actions (ST I-II, Prologue).

[11]ST I, q. 14, a. 5.

[12]Things are knowable and intelligible precisely because they proceed from a mind, the mind of God.

ourselves that leads us to confront the related mystery that there is in all other created things. Behind the knowable and lovable and beautiful, the pure of heart see God; behind the evil they see nothing.[13] Where the cynic sees through all that is beautiful and good and simple, to find murkiness within, the pure of heart see through ugliness and sin and pain and failure to find God within.

The beatitude of the pure of heart is witnessed by the authenticity of their lives.[14] The integrity of the well-ordered love that governs the pure heart is evidence of the true vision of Ultimate Reality and all related reality. The vision of the pure of heart who see God as God truly is, is born of love. God's gift of the Spirit of divine love enables us to see what we could not otherwise see and to become what we could not otherwise become. The vision born of love calls for the commitment of love to God above all and for all, which culminates in the beatific vision of the kingdom of God. This vision is the energizing source and the dynamism which bind every aspect of life into a vital synthesis; otherwise, "in the absence of vision, the people go to the dogs" (Prov 29:18).

Providentially, "The Lord takes delight in his people" (Ps 149:4). Mark's Gospel opens announcing the "beginning of the Good News about Jesus Christ, the Son of God" (1:11). The beginning of the Good News is Jesus as the Beloved of God, the one in whom God delights and in whom God's rule and kingdom are present and at work.[15] Mark presumes that the Good News is still in the process of being communicated in all who welcome the Spirit of the Beloved Son. In the Body of Christ and Temple of his Spirit, God knows divine truth, loves divine goodness, delights in divine beauty, and shares divine happiness.

Jesus' call to conversion implies that God has created the universe to make it beautiful for the divine self by reflecting God's own beauty. God, Beauty Itself, intends everything to become beautiful in the fullness of God's own beauty.[16] Jesus' call for human transformation expresses God's will to transform deformed human images of God into truly conformed human im-

[13]Simon Tugwell, O.P., *Reflections on the Beatitudes,* 96.

[14]John Navone and Thomas Cooper, *Tellers of the Word,* 68.

[15]Ibid., Appendix I: "Mark, the Model of Christian Storeyteller," 289–97.

[16]See Aquinas, *Commentary on the Divine Names,* c. 4, lect. 5, n. 349.

ages.[17] In our conformity to God's wisdom and will/love, we are beautiful living images/icons of God, irradiating God's wisdom and love.[18] Our deformity as human images/icons of God results from our resistance to God's wisdom and love. The kingdom of God is present in Jesus, the perfect image of God, whose mind and heart are perfectly conformed to the true goodness of Beauty Itself. The transfiguration or glorification of Jesus expresses what Jesus is and does for the kingdom of Beauty Itself: Jesus is transfigured and glorified humankind, Beauty Itself incarnate, transfiguring and glorifying humankind.[19] Beauty Itself, through the

[17]Aquinas describes sin as a "deformity": "All that belongs to being and action in a sinful act comes from God as first cause. But the deformity in it goes back to free will as its cause, just as the progress made by one who limps is reduced to the power of movement as its first cause, while all the obliquity in such a gait arises from the crookedness of his limbs" (*Quaestiones disputatae de potentia Dei* q. 3, a. 6, ad 20). Again: "In the demons one is aware of both their nature, which is from God, and the deformity of their sin, which is not from God. . . . But it is absolutely true to say that God is in things, if we mean things whose nature is not deformed" (ST I, q. 1 ad 4); and "Sin consists in disorder of the body" (*Quaestiones disputate de malo* 7, 1).

[18]Our likeness to God is a question of conformity: "Whoever wills something under some aspect of good, has a will conformed to the divine will" (ST I-II, q. 19, a. 10, ad 1); "Everything which strives after its own perfection tends towards likeness to God" (*Summa Contra Gentiles,* 3, 21); "The human intellect is measured by things so that our thought is not true on its own account but is called true in virtue of its conformity with things. . . . The divine intellect, on the other hand, is the measure of things, since things are true to the extent in which they represent/conform to the divine intellect" (ST I-II, q. 93, a. 1, ad 3); "The spiritual beauty of the soul consists in the fact that our conduct and action conforms with the spiritual clearness of reason" (ST II-II, q. 145, a. 2); "All creatures are nothing other than an objective expression and representation of what is contained in the concept of the divine Word" (*Summa Contra Gentiles,* 4, 42); "Knowledge and will mean that the thing known is in the knower and the thing willed/loved is in the willer/lover. Thus, according to knowledge and will/love, things are more in God than God is in things" (ST I, q. 8, a. 3, ad 3).

[19]For Dostoevsky, "there is only one face in the whole world which is absolutely beautiful: the face of Christ," and "the Incarnation is the epiphany of the Beautiful One" (*The Brothers Karamazov,* IV, 1). "Beauty will save the world," declares Dostoevsky, referring to the divine-human beauty of Jesus Christ. See Michel Quenot, *The Icon: Window on the Kingdom,* trans.

grace and call of the transfigured and transfiguring Beloved Son in whom it delights, transforms us from the ugliness of godlessness to the beauty of godliness, from the joylessness of aliens to the joyfulness of sons and daughters. The self-giving of Beauty Itself in the Beloved Son and his Spirit liberates us from the ugliness and futility of self-glorification for the beauty that is the glory of God, in which God delights.

Inasmuch as Beauty Itself is the Triune Unity, Jesus Christ's grace and call for our transfiguration into true images/icons of God entails our conformity to the unity of the Triune Community/Communion.[20] Beauty Itself is equally Goodness Itself, the Truth Itself, and the (Triune) Unity Itself. The Triune God is beautifully one, true, and good; is truly beautiful, one, and good. The One God is the supreme goodness of supreme truth and beauty in the Triune Community/Communion/Communications. We cannot, therefore, welcome the grace and call of Jesus Christ without being transfigured into a community/communion communicating in truth and goodness, the beautiful image/icon of the Triune Community/Communion which eternally communicates in knowing its truth, loving its goodness, and delighting in its beauty.[21]

A Carthusian Monk (London: Mowbray, 1992) 59, 65. Paul Evdokimov, *The Art of the Icon: A Theology of Beauty,* trans. Steven Bigham (Redondo Beach, Calif.: Oakwood Publications, 1990) v–vi: "The emptiness and the hell that has opened up in the soul of contemporary man . . . is precisely the providential place to set off the explosion of the light of the Resurrection, that is, of the Holy Spirit." Evdokimov envisions it as the explosion of the divine splendor of the beauty of God.

[20]"Just as God himself is One, so he also produces unity; not only because each being is one in itself, but also because all things in a certain sense are one perfect unity" (*Quaestiones disputatae de potentia Dei* 2, 16, 1); "The source of every imperfect thing lies necessarily in one perfect being" (*Summa Contra Gentiles* 1, 28); "What comes from God is well ordered. Now the order of things consists in this, that they are led to God each one by the others" (ST I-II, q. 111, a. 1).

[21]See Robert Kress, *The Church: Communion, Sacrament, Communication* (New York: Paulist Press, 1985). Kress sees the Church as both divine and human and points to it as a dimension of what it means to be human and as a means by which God communicates love and truth to us.

Jesus prays to his Father that all may be one as they are one (John 17:21-23). Christian unity is a requisite to manifest to all humankind God's love in giving the only Son (John 3:16) and to achieve unity in Christ (Eph 4:13). Having died and risen, Jesus communicates his Spirit for the life of his new community and the transfiguration of all humankind. In death, Jesus "gives up his Spirit" to God, and in the same act "hands on" his Spirit for the birth of the Church (John 19:30). His gift of the Spirit sustains the unity of the Church (Acts 2:42; 4:32). Jesus' gift of the Spirit inaugurates the mission of the community to continue that of Jesus: the transfiguration of all humankind. It is the power of Beauty Itself now beautifying the world in the risen glory of Jesus (John 20:21). The mission entails a liberation *from* alienation, evil, untruth, and ugliness, and a freedom *for* a universal communion in the goodness and truth and beauty of the kingdom of God (John 20:22-23). The "Trinification of the World" (title of the last chapter of Frederick E. Crowe's *The Doctrine of the Most Holy Trinity* [Toronto: Regis College] 1965) is that coming of the kingdom in which Beauty Itself, the Triune Unity, makes all things beautiful.[22]

The triune God delights in the beauty of the Triune Unity, Goodness, and Truth. Jesus delights in the beauty of his disciples' unity in true love for one another, the true image/icon of the Triune Unity, the sacrament of its transforming presence (John 13:35). The triune God delights in the beauty of its own goodness and truth uniting humankind in communion, community, and communications.

The triune God is the origin, ground, and direction or fulfillment of all human communion, community, and communications in truth and goodness. The Triune Unity creates a universe or cosmos which reflects its unity. The triune God's outward sharing begins in creation: cosmic and human nature as the image and likeness of God. It continues the salvation history as the image and likeness of God. It continues in salvation history, when God calls the covenant-community of Israel into existence. It intensifies in the incarnation of God's Son and Word in a human na-

[22]See Thomas A. Dunne and Jean-Marc Laporte, eds., *Trinification of the World: A Festschrift in Honour of Frederick E. Crowe* (Toronto: Regis College Press, 1978), Preface.

ture and matures in the Church, the body of the risen Christ and the temple of his Holy Spirit; it consummates in glorious and beatific vision: the kingdom of God, the new heaven and earth of the celestial city.[23] God's inward communion is outgoing and integrating, self-giving and embracing. The triune God's supreme happiness is itself, in its love of its absolute goodness, in its delight in its absolute beauty. The triune God does not create to get some good that it does not have, but out of the supreme happiness that it is. Creation is God's happiness in communicating and sharing the absolute goodness, truth, and beauty that God is: divine and human communication (unity) in loving and knowing and delighting.

Peace was, in the ancient Church, a synonym for communion.[24] They often appeared together as a doublet. Sometimes "peace" alone indicated the community, the communion of saints, the Church. According to St. Paul, "Christ . . . is the peace between us (Jews and Gentiles), and has made the two into one and broken down the barriers which used to keep them apart, actually destroying in his person the hostility . . . to create one single new man both in a single body and reconcile them with God. In his own person . . . he came to bring the good news of peace, peace to you who were far away and peace to those who were near at hand. Through him both of us have in the one Spirit our way to come to the Father" (Eph 2:13-18). This peace, which happens in Jesus Christ, is communion of God with humanity and of human beings among themselves. This peace continues in Jesus' gift of his Spirit as a lasting *way* to the Father. Not only is Jesus "the Way, the Truth, and the Life" (John 14:6); so is the Church. St. Paul affirms: "It is according to the way which they describe as a sect that I worship the God of my ancestors . . ." (Acts 24:14). In the peace of the Body of Christ, Paul enjoys the *shalom* of his ancestors . . ." (Acts 24:14). This passage from Ephesians locates ecclesial communion in the Triune Communion.[25] As body of Christ and temple of his Spirit, the ecclesial commun-

[23]Robert Kress, *The Church,* 2. The divine Triune Communion is in communion with the human communion which is its creation.

[24]Ludwig von Hertling, *Communio. Chiesa e papato nellantichità Cristiana* (Rome: Gregorian University, 1961) 7–9.

[25]Robert Kress, *The Church,* 36.

ion is the beautiful image/icon of the triune God sharing the divine life with human beings. It is the work of God, the "Trinification of the world," through the gift of the Son and Spirit.

The triune God's self-giving entails an ongoing transformation from chaos to cosmos or wholeness of life in a new creation. Taking a hint from the first verse of Genesis, we note that in the beginning there was not life but chaos, there was not order (form) but the formless void, the abyss of darkness.[26] Chaos represents something not yet formed and shaped into life, something lacking distinctiveness and identity. When God creates the world, God gives "cosmos" to chaos; God gives form and order and beauty to the unformed and disordered and ugly. God creates light to dispel the abyss of darkness, and to illuminate creation. God brings something beautiful to be. Inasmuch as creation stands unfinished, God continues to call us from chaos to cosmos, from formlessness to the resplendent form of God's true images. The Holy Spirit conforms our hearts and minds to God and makes us the friends of God, who delight in communion with God. The Holy Spirit, the Comforter, brings us the peace and joy of God which the world cannot give and cannot take from us (John 14:26). Through the gift of the Spirit, God enables us to become something beautiful, noble, and good that we could not otherwise become. God enables the triumph of the Triune Unity's love over the void of meaninglessness and lovelessness. God's love will complete the transformation that God's love began. John Macquarrie's paraphrase of the Prologue to John's Gospel states the case for God's ultimate triumph:

> Fundamental to everything is meaning. Meaning is closely connected with what men call "God," and, indeed, meaning and God are the same. To say that God was in the beginning is to say that there was meaning in the beginning. All things were made meaningful, and there was nothing that was made meaningless. Life was the drive towards meaning and life emerged into the light of humanity, the bearer of meaning. And meaning shines out through the threat of absurdity, for absurdity has not destroyed it. Every man has a share in the true meaning of things. This follows from

[26]See Enda McDonagh, *Between Chaos and New Creation* (Wilmington, Del.: Michael Glazier, 1990).

> the fact that this meaning has been embodied in the world from the beginning and has given the world its shape. Yet the world has not recognized the meaning. Even man, the bearer of meaning, has rejected it. But those who have received it and believed in it have been enabled to become the children of God. And this has happened not in the natural course of evolution or through human striving, but through an act of God. For the meaning has been incarnated in a human existent, in whom was grace and truth; and we have seen in him the final meaning or glory towards which everything moves—the glory of man and the glory of God (John 1:1-5, 9-14).[27]

Luke's Gospel (chapter 15) affirms that we have a God who cannot know peace until all of us share God's peace; that God is restless until God's happiness is our own. God's abiding intention is to make sure that all of us live the love, joy, and peace that is God. God is the goodness and beauty constitutive of our happiness. Although God is a goodness and beauty forever beyond us, God's love poured out in our hearts enables us to live the love, joy, and peace that is God. The gift of God's love in the Spirit transfigures and glorifies us, liberating us from one kind of self to become another shaped in God's goodness and resplendent of God's beauty. Each of us born from grace is called to glory.

God calls us to glory through the strategy of God's created universe. God's desire for our glorification and wholeness is structured into our human nature. We often seek this glory inadvertently as we grope for wholeness, but we are not sure how it is attained, or when our restlessness is searching for a peace we are not sure can be found. This is God at work in us, leading us, loving us, driving us on, persuading us not to be content until some yet-to-be-recognized joy can be ours. This is the silent presence of God in our lives to which C. S. Lewis alludes in his description of the Christian way:

> The Christian Way.—The Christian says, "Creatures are not born with desires unless satisfaction for those desires exists. A baby feels hunger: well, there is such a thing as food. A duckling wants to

[27] John Macquarrie, "Word and Idea," informally published paper given at the International Lonergan Conference (St. Leo, Florida, 1970) 7.

> swim: well, there is such a thing as water. Men feel sexual desire: well, there is such a thing as sex. If I find in myself a desire which no experience in this world can satisfy, the most probable explanation is that I was made for another world. If none of my earthly pleasures satisfy it, that does not prove that the universe is a fraud. Probably earthly pleasures were never meant to satisfy it, but only to arouse it, to suggest the real thing. If that is so, I must take care, on the one hand, never to despise, or be unthankful for, these earthly blessings, and on the other, never to mistake them for the something else of which they are only a kind of copy, or echo, or mirage. I must keep alive in myself the desire for my true country, which I shall not find till after death; I must never let it get snowed under or turned aside; I must make it the main object of life to press on to that other country and to help others to do the same."
>
> There is no need to be worried by facetious people who try to make the Christian hope of "Heaven" ridiculous by saying they do not want "to spend eternity playing harps." The answer to such people is that if they cannot understand books written for grown-ups, they should not talk about them. All the scriptural imagery (harps, crowns, gold, etc.) is, of course, a merely symbolical attempt to express the inexpressible. Musical instruments are mentioned because for many people (not all) music is the thing known in the present life which most strongly suggests ecstasy and infinity. Crowns are mentioned to suggest the fact that those who are united with God in eternity share His splendour and power and joy. Gold is mentioned to suggest the timelessness of Heaven (gold does not rust) and the preciousness of it. People who take these symbols literally might as well think that when Christ told us to be like doves, He meant that we were to lay eggs.[28]

Human beings are creatures with purpose, cares, loves, and concerns. Everything we do, even our relaxation, seems to be for a purpose. We act because we are seeking; we do things for some goal we are set to achieve. Our lives are taken up with and identified through all the purposes we have. That we are purposeful means that what we have desired we hope to see fulfilled: that we are incomplete. We act because there is something we want that we do not have. Our actions are born of need.[29] If we were

[28] C. S. Lewis, *Mere Christianity* (New York: Macmillan, 1952) 118–19.

[29] Paul J. Wadell, C.P., *The Primacy of Love* (New York: Paulist Press, 1992) 30–32.

already whole or self-sufficient, there would be no need to act. Our most perduring intention is to achieve a wholeness through the pursuit of something we hope will complete us. This becomes our sovereign love; our desire for it finds expression in all that we do. It is the love that most determines what we become. Embracing all our particular needs and desires is a comprehensive and profoundly personal need for peace, love, and abiding joy. We realize, however dimly, that there must be some radically satisfying good, the good in which we desire no more. We live in need of a completion that we can only receive, and it is through the endless forms of God's self-giving love that we receive it.[30] God calls us to live with the greatest expectations and the hope that enables us to sustain them. To believe in or hope for anything less is to reject God's will/love for us in the denial that what God wants for us can be ours. If God wants our transfiguration in godliness, hope enables us to want the same. Such glory does not occur without the gift of God's Spirit that completes what our goodness could never achieve.[31] Such glory is the work of a lifetime, ours as well as God's. When God's Spirit dwells freely within us, God is able to love and bless us as the friends that God has always desired us to become. God fully alive in us is both the perfection of truly human beauty and the glory of God. The friends of God manifest Beauty Itself, the eternal love of the triune God.

If we are created from Goodness and Beauty Itself, we return to It by loving and delighting in It, by centering our lives in It and making Its love and delight the abiding intention of our lives. If the love and delight of friendship for God is in our hearts, everything we do irradiates it as the glory of God's heartfelt meaning and presence. Our lives manifest and proclaim our sovereign love and delight, the goodness and beauty constitutive of our happiness. We invariably become what we most love and delight in as the core focus and direction of our lives. Our radical shaping/formation as one kind of person instead of another depends on the core intention of our knowing and loving, decision and action. Our character takes the shape/form of the choices that

[30]Ibid., 146.
[31]Ibid., 148.

we have made in response to our sovereign love and delight.[32] As relational beings, we inevitably manifest what we have freely chosen to relate to as our sovereign love and delight.[33] Self-idolatry is a futile attempt at self-glorification, at substituting ourselves for the Supreme Good and Beauty. Choosing to love and delight in ourselves above all implies our rejection of true love and delight.

The human ego is not the ultimate context of all human life, despite all our futile attempts to act as if it were.[34] The pedagogy of Jesus Christ and his community assumes that true love means loving others as they truly are: "God alone is good" (Mark 10:18); therefore, "Love the Lord your God with all your heart, with all your soul, with all your mind, and with all your strength" (Mark 12:29-30); secondly, "Love your neighbor as yourself" (Mark 12:31). Only when we love God above all do we know the delight of loving God as God truly is. We frustrate ourselves when we attempt to love God for less than God is, for no other is absolutely lovable/supremely good. No other can satisfy the human heart. We frustrate ourselves when we attempt to love ourselves above all; for we are not absolutely lovable or delightful. Self-idolatry precludes the joy of truly loving the limited, finite, and relational persons that we are both as individuals and as humankind. Our attempts at self-glorification bespeak both our blindness to the glory of God as the ultimate perfection to which all creation is ordered—Beauty, Truth, and Goodness Itself—and our inability to delight in it.

We cannot be truly good unless we stand in the right relation to the Common/Supreme Good of all creation.[35] Similarly, we cannot be truly beautiful as persons unless we stand in the right relation to the Supreme Beauty/Common Good of the universe. In this respect, the distinction between true beauty and seductive beauty is relevant.[36] The distinction is analogous to Aristotle's

[32]John Finnis, *Fundamentals of Ethics* (Washington, D.C.: Georgetown University Press, 1984) 29–30.

[33]Wadell, *The Primacy of Love,* 35–36.

[34]John Navone, "Divine and Human Conflict," *Priests and People* 4/3 (March 1990) 91.

[35]ST I-II, q. 92, a. 1, ad 3.

[36]Aquinas remarks that "Prudence rules the things that are ordered to wisdom, namely the means by which we ought to arrive at wisdom. In this way

distinction between prudence and cleverness. Both the prudent and the clever enjoy a facility for recognizing and choosing the means required for the attainment of their ends; however, the prudent seek moral ends, and the clever seek immoral ends. The prudent advance towards their authentic self-fulfillment; the clever proceed toward their moral and spiritual self-destruction. Similarly, true beauty entails whatever allures us to our self-fulfillment; seductive beauty entails whatever allures us to our self-destruction. The same distinction holds for our true good as opposed to an apparent good; for true love as opposed to a disordered/unwise love; for true communion/community as opposed to a counterfeit communion/community (e.g., racist and/or criminal organizations).

If true love is fidelity, responsibility, and commitment to the truly good, true joy is delight in the irradiant beauty of the truly good. The beauty or glory of God is known whenever God's goodness and truth inspire, transform, motivate, attract, and delight us. We affirm the beauty and glory of God as *Mysterium tremendum et fascinans* because the manifestations of God's true goodness delight and inspire us. We are fascinated (drawn, allured, attracted) or transformed by *Mysterium fascinans,* by manifestations of Supreme Beauty's true goodness.

The triune God is Eternal Happiness in being one/community/communion/communications in goodness, truth, and beauty. The triune God conforms us to the divine by making us one with the divine self in goodness, truth, and beauty. Through the gift of God's Spirit we share the triune God's happiness in being one/community/communion/communications in goodness, truth, and beauty. We delight with the triune God in the beauty of our being one/communion/community in knowing our truth and loving our goodness. We delight in the beauty of the triune God's eternal happiness. Boris Bobinskoy affirms that the truth of God reveals itself to us in its incarnate Beauty:

> That Truth of Christ, namely His vivifying presence, we all carry within us. According to the charism imparted to each one of us,

---

prudence is the servant of wisdom'' (ST I-II, q. 66, a. 5, ad 1); and ''Prudence considers the ways by which we arrive at beatitude'' (ST I-II, q. 66, a. 5, ad 2).

> we are called to cultivate that Truth which reveals itself to us in its Beauty, its Word of Life, consolation, judgement, edification . . . it is the Beauty of God we sense beckoning us, introducing us into His presence . . . the very Beauty of God invites us to contemplate in silence.[37]

The Beauty of God, Michael Quenot asserts, transfigures the world with joy:

> The love of beauty . . . enriches us and fills us with joy. Such beauty streams forth from God—who is Beauty itself—generating the world with divine energies. In Him alone do we discover the beauty of everything. We must plunge into the silence and depths of our own hearts in order to listen to the heartbeat of a world already transfigured.[38]

The beauty of this transfigured world requires an interior light for whoever would contemplate it: "One must welcome the Light which is God Himself (John 1:9; 8:12), so that with purified eyes, one may gaze upon the splendor of Tabor which transfigures the material world."[39] God enlightens our minds to see and inspires our hearts to delight in the all-encompassing beauty of the divine.

"In thy light do we see light" (Ps 36:9) expresses one aspect of our letting God be God, for "God is light" (1 John 1:5). The light of God enables us to see and delight in God with a true vision and love of ourselves, others, and the world. The biblical image of light implies the radiant goodness and truth and beauty of a God whose self-giving gives value and meaning and delight to humankind. Jesus' criticism of those who have eyes but do not see implies that we are free to reject or turn away from the radiant goodness and truth and beauty of God, closing our eyes to the light that is God. Athanasius, for example, interprets the Fall as a failure to see God and the things of God.[40] When Adam and Eve diverted their gaze from the light of God to themselves in

[37]Boris Bobinskoy, "Preface" to Michael Quenot, *The Icon: Window on the Kingdom,* 8. Bobinskoy qualifies the icon as being "a portal to the glory and beauty promised to us, a grandeur and beauty of which we receive a foretaste within the living experience of the Church" (7).

[38]Quenot, *The Icon,* 12.

[39]Ibid., 13.

[40]*Oratio contra gentes* 3, MPG 26, 905.

the lust of their narcissism, they recognized their nakedness (Gen 3:7). They no longer saw and loved themselves in the light of God's radiant goodness, truth, and beauty.

Fiat lux afforded Christian theologians from the very outset with an image for speaking at the same time about the nature of God as such and about the meaning of God's creative action. God is light, and God is being. Darkness is the realm of nonbeing: the absence of the one, good, true, and beautiful. When we treat nonbeing as though it were being, reversing the roles of darkness and light, we give to darkness a power over ourselves that does not belong to it. Darkness is able to usurp this power because of the false faith of all who deliberately shut their eyes against the light of being (truth, goodness, and beauty). The threat of sin is the danger that we be dragged, or voluntarily slide, back into the nonbeing from which we were originally created; that we lose touch with goodness and truth and beauty.

God, uncreated light, affects the world by irradiating it. Because God is light, the Son of God is the radiance of God, illuminating the universe. The epiphany of Christ takes place in light and splendor (Matt 17:2; Acts 9:3). Jesus is recognized as "A light for the illumination of the nations" (Luke 2:32). His impact is described in terms of light: "The people who sat in darkness saw a great light" (Matt 4:16). As children of God, his disciples are "children of the light" (Luke 16:8). Inasmuch as his disciples communicate the light they have received, they are "the light of the world" (Matt 5:14-16).

Paul affirms that God made light at the creation of the world; it shone forth on the face of Christ: "God who said, 'Out of the darkness let light shine,' has shone in our hearts as the bright light of the knowledge of the glory of God that shines on the face of Christ" (2 Cor 4:6). Christ, in his glory, is the "image of God"; preaching is "the light of the gospel of the glory of Christ" (2 Cor 4:4). Christ is the day (Rom 13:12). In preaching and sacrament Christ streams forth as light (Eph 5:14). Those who once were in darkness are now "light in the Lord" (Eph 5:8). The divine gift of light turns the faithful into light: "You are the children of the light and of day" (1 Tim 5:5).

In the Prologue of John's Gospel, Christ, the Logos/Word, is the light and life of all humankind. Light and darkness are the divine world and the world is hostile to God (1:4-5). Light is the strength of life: "The true light that enlightens everyone came into the world (in Christ)" (John 1:9). Christ himself affirms: "I am the light of the world. Whoever follows me will not walk in the darkness, but will have the light of life" (John 8:12). Christ is the light, and he gives the light that is prerequisite for communion with God. When John exhorts us to walk in the light (1 John 1:6-7), he summons us to a life free of sin and darkness. Since the light is identical with the truth (1 John 1:6), and truth is the reality of God made accessible in revelation, the light is to be apprehended in faith. Those who walk in the light have communion with God and with one another. The opposition of darkness and light represents the opposition of hatred and love: "Whoever hates his brother is in the darkness; but whoever loves his brother is in the light" (1 John 2:9-10).

5

In the Light of God's Beauty

The Platonist tradition, from Plato's dialogues to Plotinus' *Enneads,* focuses on beauty. The elevation of the soul begins with the contemplation of earthly beauty, whence the soul ascends progressively to spiritual beauty, arriving finally at the beauty of the One who is also the Good and the Beautiful. Christian theological traditions indebted to Plato have readily integrated the notion and the experience of beauty into their theology.

One of Augustine's early writings was a treatise on beauty, *De pulchro et apto (On the Beautiful and the Fitting).* This treatise has been lost, but Augustine mentions in the *Confessions* (397/401) that it made a distinction between what is beautiful in itself *(pulchrum)* and what is rendered beautiful by its harmonious setting in a wider context *(aptum).*[1] Augustine also wrote a treatise on order (*De ordine,* 386) and one on music (*De musica,* ca. 387/390), both of which deal with aspects of the beautiful. The *Confessions* express Augustine's longing for the beauty of God: "Too late have I loved you, Beauty so old and so new."[2] God's beauty is utterly attractive and, when perceived, totally satisfying. Augustine's desire for the beauty of God is related to his basic division of reality into two realms: the things that are to be used *(uti);* and the things that are to be enjoyed *(frui).*[3] Utility

[1]St. Augustine, *Confessions* IV, 15.

[2]St. Augustine, *Confessions* X, 27.

[3]St. Augustine, *De doctrina christiana* I, 2 (translated *Christian Instruction,* in *Writings of St. Augustine,* The Fathers (New York: Cima Pub., 1947) 28–29.

is a matter of technique; fruition is reached through contemplation. As supremely enjoyable Being, God alone can be contemplated as totally beautiful. In his journey from Manichaeism to Christianity, Augustine learned that God has brought divine beauty near to us in the incarnate Word; by grace, the beauty of Christ can be shared by the faithful. Therefore, his long inquiry into the nature of *The City of God* (413 to 426) could properly end on a discussion of the beauty of Christ and of the risen bodies of the saints.[4]

Hans Urs von Balthasar has shown that the perception of the glory of God has inspired the Christian search for Beauty Itself. He sees the history of Christian theology as a history of attempts to express the glory of God in successive styles and theories of beauty.[5]

From St. Gregory Nazianzen (327–90) and Boethius (ca. 480–524) to St. Thomas Aquinas, through innumerable patristic and medieval authors, poetry expressed the sense of beauty that was inseparable from the perception of the divine. The sense of God's beauty is central to the *Spiritual Canticle* of John of the Cross: "Let us rejoice, Beloved, and let us go see ourselves in your beauty" (stanza 35 in version A; stanza 36 in version B). The Mystical Doctor gave a major place to the beauty of God in both his poems and in his theological commentaries.

The distinguished philosopher and theologian Nicholas of Cusa (1401–64) recommended focusing attention on a picture of the holy face of Jesus as the initial step toward Christian contemplation.[6] In the Orthodox Church, a nonverbal theology—expressed, taught, and experienced through icons—reached official status.

[4]St. Augustine, *The City of God* XXII, 19.

[5]Hans Urs von Balthasar, *Herrlichkeit,* 8 vols. (Einsiedeln: Johannes Verlag, 1961–68). This is the first part of a trilogy; it is followed by a study of divine drama, *Theodramatik,* 4 vols. (Einsiedeln: Johannes Verlag, 1963–83) and of divine logic, *Theologik,* 3 vols. (Einsiedeln: Johannes Verlag, 1985–87). Some volumes of *Herrlichkeit* have been translated into English: *The Glory of the Lord: A Theological Aesthetics,* vol. 1; *Seeing the Form* (San Francisco: Ignatius Press, 1984); vol. 2: *Studies in Theological Styles: Clerical Styles* (San Francisco: Ignatius Press, 1984); vol. 3: *Studies in Theological Styles: Lay Styles* (San Francisco: Ignatius Press, 1986).

[6]Nicholas of Cusa, *The Vision of God* (New York: Ungar, 1960) 1–6.

The Gothic art and architecture of the West were justified theologically, in the line of the great mystics and theologians of St. Victor, Hugh (1096–1140) and Richard (1104–73), by the builder of the first Gothic church, Suger (ca. 1081–1151), the abbot of St. Denys. Following St. Bernard's conceptions of spiritual aesthetics, a form of Gothic art that was bare of ornamentation came to characterize the constructions of the Cistercian Order.[7]

Theologians commonly associated the perception of beauty with seeing and hearing. St. Bonaventure associated beauty with hearing music: "The whole of Scripture is like a zither, and the lower string does not create harmony by itself, but in common with the others."[8] Beauty is associated with sight in Ezekiel's description of the Temple in chapters 40–43, and in the Book of Revelation's description of the walls of the New Jerusalem (21:10-23). Church architecture, painting, sculpture, and music imply the relationship of sight and sound in the Christian community's approach to divine beauty.

St. Bonaventure employed the symbol of light in his theological approach to beauty. He reflected the medieval theologians' use of light as a central symbol for the transcendental and actual beauty of creatures. Light as such is not seen; one only sees lighted objects. Likewise, we do not see beauty, but beautiful objects. The creed of Nicaea—Constantinople's statement that the divine Word is "light from light"—encouraged the use of light as a Christian symbol for the divine beauty and for the radiation of the divine glory. Readers of the Bible have always appreciated the wealth of religious meaning conveyed by the symbol of light. The psalmist affirms that "In your light we see light" (36:9); and the New Testament echoes this same theme when it declares that "God is light" (1 John 1:5). The light of the world is a basic image in early Christian thought.[9]

[7]George H. Tavard, *Juana Inés de la Cruz and the Theology of Beauty* (Notre Dame: University of Notre Dame Press, 1991) 189.

[8]St. Bonaventure, *Collationes in Hexaemeron* XIX, 7. Bonaventure invokes four transcendentals and links them to the causes: unity to the efficient cause, truth to the formal cause, goodness to the final cause, and beauty to all the causes. Beauty presupposes the other transcendentals; and as a consequence, the causes associated with each of them.

[9]Jaroslav Pelikan, *The Light of the World: A Basic Image in Early Christian Thought* (New York: Harper, 1962). Albert the Great associated beauty

Light (radiance, clarity) is related to form in St. Thomas' theology of beauty; and form is related to existence and action.

The existence, form, and action of a being are the components and ground of its beauty. Existence, innermost in everything, is the secret source of all the perfection and actuality of a being, including its beauty.[10] Form or structure is whatever determines whatever exists in its kind and species; it makes it what it is and also distinguishes it from beings of other species.[11] Action completes the actuality of existence and form.[12] A singer asleep, for example, is still a singer, but is most completely a singer when actually singing. If beauty is found in actuality, its fullness will be found in action.

Form is central to beauty, for things stand out for us by their forms. They are the aspects under which things appear to us and by which we recognize them. Because forms enlighten us as to what things are, we think of a form as a kind of light to which we must attend if we are to perceive or understand a thing. Form, for Aquinas, is ultimately a participation in the divine radiance because the Creator knows in the luminosity of the divine mind what is created.[13]

Each form has its own light, radiance, clarity or splendor which it imparts to the being of which it is the form.[14] In this sense the

---

with goodness in a moral sense, and connected it with truth or wisdom as the source of light and form. He describes the effect of the contemplation of beauty as illumination, brought about by light and beauty (*De bono* 1.2.1–2). Beauty, he says in his *Summa theologica* (1.6.26.2.3) pertains to the perfection of a being as related to divine wisdom. The metaphysical basis for beauty is light or form. His student Ulric of Strassbourg taught that beauty is form as intelligible light (*Summa de Bono* 4.2.5); that the divine beauty contains virtually every form and, therefore, all that is created. Both Sts. Albert and Thomas hold that the beautiful is cognitively delightful (Thomas, ST I-II, q. 27, a. 1, ad 3; Albert, ST 1.6.26.1.–2.3.8a).

[10]My treatment of beauty is based on a Thomistic interpretation. ST I, q. 8, a. 1, c.

[11]*In Div. Nom.*, c. 4, *lect.* 5, no. 349, p. 114. Beauty is grounded in form (ST I, q. 5, a. 4, ad 1m).

[12]*De Potentia Dei* VII, 2 ad 9m; ST I, q. 4, a.1, ad 3m.

[13]Form is a participation in the divine radiance (*In Div. Nom.* c. 4, *lect.* 5, n. 349, p. 114. *Ibid.*, n. 360, p. 118.

[14]*In III Sent.* d. 23, q. 3, a. 1, qu. 1, *sed contra.*

form of a being gives it its beauty.[15] A physical/sensible form, like the shape or color of a flower, gives the being a physical radiance which the eye can perceive. An intelligible form, like the structure of a mathematical equation, imparts an intelligible radiance which can illuminate the mind. Each kind of form determines and specifies a being in its own way, different from every other. It thereby imparts its own kind of radiance to the being: now a physical radiance, now an intelligible or spiritual radiance. Because each being has its own form, it has its own distinctive "light" or splendor.

The effulgence or luminosity of a being is integral to its beauty because it illuminates our senses, imagination, or mind and thereby delights us. Darkness and obscurity, on the contrary, preclude the expression of beauty both to the senses and the intelligence. To the extent that an idea is unclear, it fails to delight the mind; rather, it causes irritation and displeasure and hence is lacking in beauty.[16]

Besides radiance and luminosity, harmony or proportion is essential to beauty.[17] Words, for example, have their beauty when they are arranged in an order that enables the light of reason to shine through them. Similarly, musical notes, when well orchestrated are harmonious and pleasing to the ear.[18] The same is true of human actions, which have a spiritual beauty because they are well disposed through the light of reason.[19] Appropriate behavior attracts; boorish behavior repels.

The beauty of one thing is not the beauty of another; for beauty is relative to the subject of beauty.[20] The proportion that is essential to beauty is analogous. Wherever there is unity in variety there is proportion, but the mode of proportion differs in each case. Similarly, beauty is the harmony of the members of a body

[15]ST I, q. 5, a. 4, ad 1m.

[16]Armand A. Maurer, C.S.B. *About Beauty* (Houston: University of St. Thomas, 1983) 10.

[17]See ST I, q. 5, a. 4, ad 1m; I, q. 39, a. 8; II-II, q. 145, a. 2. As radiance comes from form, so proportion or harmony comes from the ordering of a thing to an end (See *In Div. Nom.*, n. 367, p. 119).

[18]*In Div. Nom.*, n. 349, p. 114.

[19]See ST I, q. 39, a. 8.

[20]*In Psalmos,* xliv, 2, p. 504.

or of colors/sounds, but the harmony of the one is different from that of the other.

Beauty, besides radiance and proportion, requires wholeness or integrity.[21] What is beautiful is integral or whole; it lacks nothing, taking into account the sort of thing that it is. It is complete or integral in both its being and operation/action.[22] It is ugly to the extent that it lacks any of the parts required for the perfection of its form, or fails in its perfect operation. Ugliness is the lack of beauty, as error is the lack of truth and evil the lack of goodness. It is a privation of what should be for the perfection of something or someone.[23] It is less than it should be. Something has gone wrong with it; consequently, it engenders feelings of displeasure, revulsion, or even fright.

As there is both physical and spiritual beauty, so there is a corresponding physical and spiritual ugliness.[24] A severely scarred face, music too loud, and therefore out of proportion to the human ear—these strike us as sensibly displeasing and ugly. Actions that fail to display the light of human reason, like cruelty or murder, affront the human mind. We call them ugly deeds. Whether the ugliness concerns the physical externals of a thing or its inner intelligible makeup, it is always the absence of due radiance, order or integrity. It is never a positive trait.[25]

If there is a truth and goodness and beauty of things, there is respectively a knowing and loving and delighting cause for it. The Creator of all things, according to the biblical tradition of faith, truly knows and loves and delights in whatever is created. Because

[21]See ST I, q. 39, a. 8.

[22]*In IV Sent.* d. 26, q. 2, a. 4.

[23]See *In Div. Nom.*, c. 4, *lect.* 21, n. 554, p. 206; ST I, q. 39, a. 8, c.

[24]*Contra Impugnantes Dei Cultum et Religionem,* c. 7, ad 9m; *Opuscula Omnia,* ed. Mandonnet (Paris, 1927) 4:118–19.

[25]Though ugliness, like evil, is a defect in being, it can, by contrast to beauty, enhance it. Ugliness and evil fall under God's providence, not in themselves *(per se),* but *per accidens.* Aquinas writes that if evil were removed from some parts of the universe, much perfection would perish from the universe, whose beauty arises from an ordered unification of evil and good things. In fact, while evil things originate from good things that are defective, still, certain good things will result from them, as a consequence of the providence of the governor. Thus, even a silent pause makes a song appealing (See *Contra Gentiles.* III, 71, 7).

creation expresses the Creator's knowing and loving and delighting, we can lovingly and gratefully contemplate the Creator in this very Creation.

We can, with the eye of faith and love, recognize the Creator in creation, the Giver in these gifts. We can share the Creator's loving gaze on creation in our contemplation of it. The true goodness and beauty of creation draws us to Truth, Goodness, and Beauty Itself.

The biblical revelation implies that the Creator's act of creation grounds all human love and delight: "I will you to be; it is good, very good" (Gen 1:31). The Creator has already infused everything that we can love and affirm with lovability and affirmability.[26] Our love and delight, therefore, are always a retrospective participation in the Creator's.

The Greek philosophers were well aware of the connection between the good and the beautiful. Their word of beautiful *(kalos)* also means the good, the right, the noble. Their word comes from the verb *kaleo,* which means "to call." Both the good and the beautiful call or beckon us. They attract us so that we want to make them a part of our lives. The beauty of the truly good evokes or calls for our joy and delight in it.

The things that we find good and beautiful call us beyond themselves to an ever more perfect goodness and beauty. They do not, in themselves, completely satisfy us; for every creature is limited, partial, changeable, and variable.[27] We long for a beauty that is full, complete, and lasting: God or Beauty Itself. In our experience of being grasped by the beautiful, we are implicitly aware of the chasm that lies between a particular embodiment of beauty in which we delight and the unlimited beauty for which we long in the depths of our desire, a delight forever.

Scripture's metaphors of hearing and seeing imply how the Eternal Word/Light/Love/Beauty, by which all things are created, sustained, and drawn to their fulfillment, transforms or beautifies humankind.

If hearing the Word of God means treasuring, obeying, and conforming to the grace and call of Beauty Itself, it also means

[26]Josef Pieper, *About Love,* trans. Richard and Clara Winston (Chicago: Franciscan Herald Press, 1974) 25.

[27]*In Div. Nom.,* ibid., n. 345, p. 114.

the beautiful resonance of that word in the lives of those who hear it. Jesus alludes to persons in harmony with the truth and goodness of that word as his mother, brothers, and sisters.

The happiness of all who have ears to hear the word of God is linked with that of all who have eyes to see the beauty of its true meaning and goodness in Jesus Christ.

As the Light of the World, Jesus enables us to see the splendor of God's loving kindness embracing and beautifying the world. His giving sight to the blind reveals that he enables our true vision. As Savior, he liberates us from the impediments to our hearing and seeing and rejoicing in the loving Creator, Sustainer, and Fulfillment of that world as our Father. Through the gift of the Spirit, we are enabled to recognize a cosmos in which all things are working for our good (Rom 8:28); we are blessed with the assurance of a God-given fulfillment beyond the best that we could ever imagine for ourselves (1 Cor 2:9).

God, Beauty Itself, beautifies the world through the Word God speaks and the Light God irradiates in the body of Christ and the temple of the Spirit. Enlightened by the Word and loved by the Spirit, all creation irradiates the true loveliness of the Triune God, Beauty Itself.

The beauty of God's self-giving love in Jesus Christ enables Christians to affirm that God is love and loves us; that God has sent Jesus Christ as the promised servant Messiah to unite all humankind in universal friendship under the sovereignty of God's love (cf. Isa 25:6-10). Jesus Christ and his community of faith are the sacrament of the Eternal Love which beautifies the world.

The great commandment, to love God above all and others as ourselves, expresses the grace and call of God for the beauty of humankind in the fullness of divine and human friendship. The Eternal Word/Light/Love/Beauty has given all creation a good and beautiful order where beings are ordered to each other as well as to God. In fact, the order of the parts of creation to each other exists in virtue of the order of the whole of creation (the universe) to God. It is through the beauty of the created order of things that they are led to God each one by the others. Human finitude is the possibility of reciprocity in that no one is self-sufficient for the achievement of one's perfection or happiness. We are free to accept or reject ourselves as we truly are: as known and loved *together* in the triune communion of Eternal Love.

God wills/loves us in our togetherness with all others. We are together-with-all-others because that is the way the Eternal Word/Light/Love/Beauty wills/loves to make all things beautiful/lovely.[28]

[28]John Navone, "Pre-Renaissance Franciscan and Tuscan Humanism," *New Blackfriars* 75 (no. 882, May 1994) 274:

> In the universities, the scholastic philosophers of the thirteenth century never discussed "art" as such. They did, however, consider the meaning of beauty, and elaborated a well-considered and perhaps influential aesthetic. Treatments of the theme all derived ultimately from a Latin version of the treatise *On the Beautiful* by the early sixth century writer, Dionysius the Pseudo-Areopagite. They are to be found in Albert the Great's *Opusculum de Pulchro,* in the *Summa de Bono* of Ulrich of Strassbourg, and in the *Summa Theologiae* of St. Thomas. The views of Aquinas may be taken as typical. The beauty of an object or creature is only a likeness or symbol *(similitudo)* of that divine beauty in which all things participate. Thus in one sense, the beautiful and the good and the true are one. Yet in another sense, that of logical priority, they are different, for beauty adds to the cognitive faculty by which the good is known as such. Beauty then is the means by which truth is seen to be truth, and so it is easy to assign to it a didactic role. To achieve it, three things are necessary—*integritas* (wholeness), *proportio sive consonantia* (proportion or harmony), and *claritas* (brightness or illumination). The canon of St. Thomas and his contemporaries demanded clear expression; it considered any vagueness as a privation of form. It looked forward to the precision and clarity which was to be a leading characteristic of Florentine and Sienese art in the following century. The scholastic contention that just measure *(commensuratio)* is indispensable for beauty makes us think of Giotto and those new conventions of reality which were about to emerge in art. Both philosophers and artists were affected at the same time by intellectual, social and religious developments.

6

The Christian Experience of Beauty

The Christian experience of beauty, as affirmed in our introduction, is always a faith experience and, as such, has its presuppositions. One such presupposition is that God gives God's self to us in all our experience; for God not only creates but also sustains and calls to perfection all creation. Another presupposition of our Christian faith-principle of interpreting all our experience is that our self-giving God is Goodness and Truth and Beauty Itself. Such faith not only inspired St. Ignatius of Loyola to speak of "seeing God in all things" but also of seeing God's love for us in all things. Ignatius saw Love/Goodness Itself serving us in all creation with the same Christian faith-principle of interpretation that enabled Paul to see that "in everything God works for good with those who love Him, who are called according to His purpose" (Rom 8:28). For those who love God the splendor of God's loving kindness is "visible" in all experience. Both Paul and Ignatius affirm that the eye of Christian faith/love perceives the splendor of Goodness and Truth and Beauty Itself in all things working for our good.

Because love can grow cold, the lifelong process of Christian conversion/experience is precarious. We can, regrettably, lose the love/faith that entails the joyful vision/experience of Love Itself in all things.

A final note on the nature of Christian religious experience may help to clarify the meaning of "seeing God in all things." The theological insights of Bernard Lonergan and Simon Tugwell are especially helpful in our attempts at clarification.

Both religious and Christian conversion entail religious experience. What Lonergan, therefore, affirms about religious conversion holds for Christian conversion and experience.

Religious conversion, for Lonergan, is being grasped by ultimate concern.[1] It is otherworldly falling in love, total and permanent self-surrender without conditions, qualifications, reservations: not as an act, but as a dynamic state that is prior to and the principle of subsequent acts. Religious conversion is theocentric self-transcendence. When religious conversion transforms the human subject into a subject in love, held, grasped, possessed, owned through a total and otherworldly love, the human capacity for self-transcendence meets fulfillment and the human desire for self-transcendence turns to joy. This transformation of the cognitive and affective consciousness of the human subject provides a new basis for valuing and doing good. Religious conversion is interpreted differently in the context of different religious traditions. For Christians it is God's love flooding our hearts through the Holy Spirit given to us. The Christian principle of community conjoins the inner gift of God's love at the heart of religious conversion with its outer manifestation in Christ Jesus and in those who follow him at the heart of Christian conversion.[2] Christian conversion is a Christocentric theocentricity, a cognitive and affective communion with the Spirit of Jesus Christ and his Father in the Christian community of faith.[3]

Religious experience, Lonergan affirms, spontaneously manifests itself in changed attitudes, in that harvest of the Spirit that is love, joy, peace, kindness, goodness, fidelity, gentleness, and self-control.[4] But it is also concerned with its base and focus in the *mysterium fascinans et tremendum* that is common to world religions such as Christianity, Judaism, Islam, Zoroastrian Mazdaism, Hinduism, Buddhism, Taoism. Lonergan notes Friedrich

[1]Bernard Lonergan, *Method in Theology* (London: Darton, Longman and Todd, 1972) 240–41.

[2]Ibid., 360.

[3]The Trinitarian character of Christian religious experience is clear in Paul's description of the community of faith as "the body of Christ" and as "the temple of the Spirit." Christians worship or "know God" (in the biblical sense) in communion with the body of his Son and the temple of their Spirit.

[4]Lonergan, *Method,* 108.

Heiler's description of seven common areas in the experience of such religions.[5] All agree that there is a transcendent reality; that it is immanent in human hearts; that it is supreme beauty, truth, righteousness, goodness; that it is love, mercy, compassion; that the way to it is repentance, self-denial, prayer; that the way is love of one's neighbor, even of one's enemies; that the way is love of God, so that bliss is conceived as knowledge of God, union with God, or dissolution into God.

These seven common features of world religions, for Lonergan, are implicit in the experience of being in love in an unrestricted manner.[6] To be in love without qualifications or conditions or limits is to be in love with someone transcendent. When someone transcendent is my beloved, he is in my heart, real to me from within me. When that love is the fulfillment of my unrestricted thrust to self-transcendence through intelligence and truth and responsibility, the one that fulfills that thrust must be supreme in intelligence, truth, and goodness. Since it chooses to come to me by a gift of love for him, he himself must be love. Since loving him is my transcending myself, it also is a denial of the self to be transcended. Since loving him means loving attention to him, it is prayer, meditation, contemplation. Since love of him is fruitful, it overflows into love of all those that he loves or might love. Finally, from an experience of love focused on mystery there wells forth a longing for knowledge, while love itself is a longing for union; so for the lover of the unknown beloved, the concept of bliss is knowledge of him and union with him, however they may be achieved.

Christian religious experience is based on the possibility that God will impinge on us in our world in some way that we can apprehend. Christians believe that what God has done in Jesus Christ confirms this possibility. God approaches us personally in Jesus Christ and elicits a personal reaction from us. Although we Christians believe that Christ is at work in his Church and in his world (Matt 28:20), we know that he is nevertheless with us in a mysterious way; for we are still waiting his glorious appearing

[5]Ibid., 109. Friedrich Heiler, "The History of Religions as a Preparation for the Cooperation of Religions," *The History of Religions,* eds. M. Eliade and J. Kitagawa (Chicago: University of Chicago Press, 1959) 142–53.

[6]Ibid., 109.

(Titus 2:13). In the meantime, he is hidden and we are hidden in him: "when Christ appears, who is our life, then you too will appear with him in glory" (Col 3:3-4). There is always a depth to Christian life or experience which eludes our grasp, so that whatever conviction we may have of God's grace and intimacy, our life/experience in Christ is more than what we know. What transcends our grasp defines our lives of faith and hope and love—our response to the mystery of God in Jesus Christ, our Ultimate Context or Origin-Ground-Destiny. What forms in us true "experiential knowledge" of God is not some special kind of experience, but all that happens to us from one moment to the next within our Ultimate Context that is our Origin-Ground-Destiny. The variety of our internal experience is part of our spiritual or religious maturation, so we should not identify any particular kind of feeling or sensation with such maturation.[7] The Holy Spirit enables us to respond to the grace and call of God within the welter of our alternating feelings or experiences.

Eschatological hope is a dimension of Christian life/experience. Our complete and blissful union with God in Christ will be revealed at the end of time; it is not something that we can now fully apprehend. We should not confuse the delights we may sometimes enjoy in our faith with the final contentment that is in store for us. The unpredictability of our experience is a useful corrective; for we can never in this world see or feel more than an image of the hidden fullness of life which we have in Christ. Our religious experience, Simon Tugwell affirms, is iconic.[8] Whatever kind of experience we choose to consider may well serve to illustrate some facet of the reality of what we are, hiddenly, in Christ; but it can never be identified with the fullness of that reality.

[7]Nicholas Lash, *Theology on the Way to Emmaus* (London: SCM Press, 1986) 155. Lash rejects the notion that God is to be found in a particular sphere of our experience, say "religious experience." He also criticizes the tendency to describe "religious experience" as essentially private, inner, and subjective, as if the real "me" exists somewhere inside my head (144). Equally misguided is the notion that the personal is the individual, leading to the belief that "religious experience" consists in the feelings, acts, and experiences of individuals in their solitude, so far as they apprehend themselves to stand in relation to whatever they consider the divine (146–47).

[8]Simon Tugwell, O.P., "Faith and Experience: XII Christian Experience," *New Blackfriars* 61/717 (February 1980) 73–74.

Some people, for example, may feel "guided" to do certain things, which may or may not turn out to be obviously beneficial. Surely the first thing to say is that it is basic to Christian faith that God does guide us. All our ways are included within God's providential ordering of the universe. God is continually forming within us, by the working of the Holy Spirit, a will which is progressively brought into harmony with the divine will. Any "experience" of guidance, then, is in principle a suitable icon of this basic truth of Christian revelation. It would be true to say that we are not guided when we commit sin. But apart from that, it is far from obvious what sense we can give to the suggestion that we are acting independently of God's guidance. Even if, in retrospect, we had to conclude that we had made a mistake, we must acknowledge that all outcomes, whatsoever they may be, are part of the whole way in which God is guiding this universe to its final goal. The mistake that we are likely to make is to think that there is something specially "guided" about situations that are accompanied by certain internal sensations. The occasional feeling of being guided is better taken as a kind of icon/illustration which can make more convincing the belief that all we do, both in the short term and the ultimate outcome, is within the hands of God. Our growing sensitivity to the will of God should result in a greater fidelity to God's purposes and a greater confidence that we are living in God's friendship; but it should never be too naively identified with any particular kind of experience.[9]

People who sometimes have the sense of being comforted by the love of God may wonder whether it is simply "imagination." A basic dogma of Christian revelation is that God loves us. To sense that we are loved, therefore, is to sense something that is true.[10] It may well be that imagination is involved in our sensation, but the truth of the dogma must stand. The mistake is to identify love with the sensation, so that the cessation of the feeling is taken to mean the cessation of the love, which would be heretical. Authentically Christian experience is based on the truth

[9]Tugwell, "Faith and Experience: XII Christian Experience," 75. Tugwell finds no adequate doctrinal reason for the attempt that has been made by such theologians as Herbert Muhlen to *prescribe* experience, or for the philosophical desire to *predict* experlence.

[10]Tugwell, "Faith and Experience: XII Christian Experience," 75.

of the historical revelation of Jesus Christ. Faith in the truth of that revelation, when it becomes the principle for the interpretation of all our experience, is the indispensable condition for all authentically Christian experience. Faith in Jesus Christ and the truth of his historical revelation communicated in and by his Church is the principle of interpretation for all genuinely Christian religious experience. There is no Christian religious experience apart from this faith-principle of interpretation, empowered by the gift of the Holy Spirit to the community of the faithful. It is not important that we should have any particular experience or experiences; rather, we must learn to interpret all experience with Christian faith. Christians manifest their maturity when they interpret their experience in the light of Jesus Christ and his teaching; they disclose their immaturity when they seek a particular "religious" experience on the implicit assumption that the teaching of Jesus Christ and his community of faith do not suffice. Learning to interpret our experience in a proper doctrinal light characterizes Christian maturation.

Simon Tugwell correctly believes that the phenomenological and psychological study of mystical experiences in themselves is so unrewarding; and also believes why a comparison, simply at that level, between the mysticism of different religious systems is more likely to be misleading than helpful.[11] Both prescind from the specific faith-principle of interpretation that defines or constitutes an experience for what it is.

Whatever good that happens is a divine effect; consequently, if we feel that our lives are lacking in religious experience, it is not because some special experience is lacking, but because we have not brought our everyday experience into the context of our belief. God gives God's self in all our experience, so that everything ordinary becomes extraordinary. Interpreted in the light of Christian faith, our experience is Christian experience. Our faith in a triune God whose love encompasses all things enables us to see God in all things. Eternal bliss itself is interpreted as seeing all things with the eye of love in the beatific vision, the ultimate achievement of God's love flooding our hearts through the Holy Spirit given to us. Even now in a glass darkly the eye of Christian

[11] Tugwell, "Faith and Experience: XII Christian Experience," 76.

love proleptically enjoys something of that vision in all our experience.

There is no such thing as a brute fact; for all facts are interpreted. Similarly, there is no such thing as uninterpreted human experience; for all human experience is interpreted. Furthermore, there is no interpretation of human experience apart from a faith-principle (hypothesis, assumption) of interpretation. The cognitive-affective consciousness of interpreting human subjects is disclosed in their interpretations of experience. The self is conscious of itself as the subject of a verb that is interpretative of its experience on the basis of some faith-principle of interpretation. The believing and hoping and loving Christian self is consciously interpreting its experience of being in the world together with all others.

Every person embodies an interpretation of God, the world, others, and himself or herself that is attained in the concreteness of experience and, in turn, is expressed at every level of one's being and becoming. Human life stories are their own interpretation inasmuch as they are the product of the understanding/interpretation that people have of themselves, their situation, their role, the human condition.[12] The interpretation interprets the interpreter. Both our life story and the stories we tell express the cognitive and affective reality of our inner being: the interpreting vision that permeates our thoughts, desires, interests, ideals, imagination, feelings, and body language. Life stories are the product of our worldview, our sense of life, our basic faith, our way of grasping the complexity of life. Human stories are interpretations that provide the evidence for our interpreting their authors. By their stories we shall know them.

Christian religious experience is ecclesial. It is specified by the common faith-principle of interpretation that unites the Christian community of faith.[13] That faith is the common good in which

[12]John Navone and Thomas Cooper, *Tellers of the Word* (formerly Le Jacq, now published [1981] by Jesuit Educational Center for Human Development, Cambridge, Mass.) 51.

[13]John Navone, S.J., *History and Faith in the Thought of Alan Richardson* (London: SCM Press, 1966) 62. There is no such thing as "presuppositionless history" or human experience; some faith-principle or other is operative in all human experience.

all the members of the body of Christ share in their interpretation of human experience. It is the faith of a living and scriptural tradition that expresses Jesus Christ's interpretation of our basic relationship to ourselves, others, the world, and God.

The Christian faith-principle of interpreting human experience is that of a sacred tradition: that process of transmission and reception in and through which the identity of a revelation (information, promise, commandment) which was once imparted to humankind from God, is preserved and kept alive in the present over the course of many generations. It implies that God has spoken to a chosen few—patriarchs, prophets, apostles, and that these "inspired" individuals, the original recipients of the word of God, share this word with others. All these "others"—above all those born long after the revelatory event—partake in this divine self-disclosure.[14] The listening and the faith of the "others" are not directed toward the original recipients and witnesses of the revelation, but solely toward the One who spoke to them in time past (cf. Heb 1:1-2). Thus each successive generation, representing the last link in the chain of the sacred tradition, has the responsibility to hear and understand/interpret the original message/disclosure/faith-interpretation truly, without omitting or adding anything that might distort its meaning. Those born after the revelatory event must necessarily look toward the past to find the divine message/principle of faith-interpretation which is prior to, and a given, of their existence.

The Christian interpretation of experience constituting Christian experience accords with the divine revelation of Jesus Christ as communicated in the sacred tradition of his community of faith. It is inevitably oriented toward the future, because the content of God's word possesses the character of a promise—a promised future.[15] The gospel is a promise and a pledge of the future en-

[14]H. R. Mackintosh, *The Christian Apprehension of God* (London: SCM Press, 1929) 65, wrote that "All religious knowledge of God, wherever existing, comes by revelation; otherwise we should be committed to the incredible position that man can know God without His willing to be known." Revelation and knowledge of God belong to one another as correlatives.

[15]Josef Pieper, *Problems of Modern Faith: Essays and Addresses,* trans. Jan van Heurck (Chicago: Franciscan Herald Press, 1985) 165. "Pastless Future, Groundless Hope," the title of this essay, implies that what we be-

visaged by Jesus Christ and his community of faith. Christian worship awaits its culmination at some point in the future with the coming of the Lord at the end of time (1 Cor 11:26), and yet it is a memorial celebration in which is proclaimed the death of the Lord. The Christian faith-principle of interpretation, supremely operative in Christian worship, interprets all human experience, present and past and future.[16]

The Christian experience of beauty entails the way that we envision God. The way in which we envision God is always determined from the start by the way we love and treasure the things/persons presented to us within the context of our life's story. Human experience is both cognitive and affective. The truthfulness of our images of God, the authenticity of our knowledge of God, the maturity of our love of God, the way in which

---

lieve about the past corresponds to what we look for from the future; a tradition is an orientation for a particular future.

[16]Interpretation, according to Francis George, bishop of Yakima (*Proceedings of the American Catholic Philosophical Association, 1993,* 34–35), is a communitarian activity because it is a joining, a communion, of three poles: the interpreter, the sign or object interpreted, and the person(s) for whom the interpretation is intended, the interpretee(s). By way of example, George imagines an international conference during which speeches are translated simultaneously. The speaker's words are the sign or object interpreted; the translator is the interpreter; and those who do not understand the speaker's language are the interpretees. Together, they form a community of interpretation. Without one of the three, but especially without the interpreter, no community exists, and the conference becomes impossible. Pushing the example further, George imagines an abstruse speech which makes little sense even to those who understand the language in which it is delivered. Then another sort of interpreter is required, perhaps a teacher or clarifier, who creates community between speaker and those spoken to. George asks what might happen should even the speaker not understand his speech. He believes that the situation would probably then call for a counselor or psychiatrist, who could explain the speaker to himself or to herself. In any set of circumstances, however, the act of interpreting means that someone interprets something or someone to and for another. The "other" might be the interpreter himself or herself at a different time. Everyone, George remarks, has experienced puzzling through a conundrum and finally "interpreting" it to oneself; but even in this case there are three logically distinct subjects of the relationship: interpreter, interpreted and interpretee. Interpretation is always a communitarian activity.

we understand or envision God, will always rest upon the truthfulness of our images of contingent realities, the authenticity of our knowledge of contingent realities, the maturity with which we responsibly love finite things and persons, the way in which we understand or envision the things of this world. It is, as Karl Rahner has affirmed (*Hearers of the Word* [London: Sheed & Ward, 1969]106), not as though we first of all knew God in a *neutral* fashion, subsequently considering whether to adopt a loving or hating attitude toward this God. Such neutral knowledge of vision, such "objectivity," is a philosophical abstraction. Our Christian experience or vision of God's beauty in things and persons is born of the love and truthfulness or lack of love and truthfulness with which we relate to the persons and things presented to us within the context of our life's story.

There is a paradoxical depth-dimension to the Christian experience of beauty in superficially unattractive persons whose profound goodness outshines all else. There is also the correlative experience of human ugliness in superficially attractive persons.

Lonergan's theology of religious and Christian conversion affirms that all Christian religious experience results from God's love flooding our hearts through the Spirit given to us. This transforming love is operative in at least seven areas common to world religions. Second, there is always more to Christian religious experience than we can grasp because of its eschatological character. Third, as Tugwell asserts, because God gives God's self to us in all our experience, particular experiences are "iconic," for they illustrate/picture instances of God's self-giving. Fourth, because all experience is interpreted by some faith-principle of interpretation or other, there is no such thing as uninterpreted human experience. Wherever the Christian faith-principle of interpretation is operative (through God's love flooding our hearts) in our interpreting human experience, we have Christian religious experience. Fifth, Christian religious experience is ecclesial because our faith-principle of interpretation is the common good of the community of faith's sacred tradition. The gift of the Spirit from which that faith derives is also the common good/life of the community of faith. It is only in the light of this gift that we can even now see the splendor of Beauty Itself in all things.

The journey of the soul to Beauty Itself is always a path through intellect. According to Ewert H. Cousins, the most characteristic form of Christian mysticism is speculative (see his translation of *Bonaventure: The Soul's Journey into God; The Tree of Life; The Life of St. Francis* [New York: Paulist Press, 1978], note on speculation, 59). Cousins rightly contests the widespread assumption that spirituality deals exclusively with affectivity or devotion, or is concerned merely with growth processes, devoid of intellectual content. On the contrary, intellectual reflection is precisely the praxis of a highly speculative Christian spirituality which cannot be separated from speculative theology.

The Church's catechesis enlightens the journey of the Christian community to Beauty Itself. The Church's evangelization and catechesis help us to live ever more fully within the holy and loving mystery of God. Evangelization leads to encounter with Christ, conversion of heart, and the experience of the Holy Spirit in the community of the Church. Catechesis goes beyond evangelization. It consists in everything which the Church does to bring faith to maturity. This is a never-ending process.

The effective catechesis of the Church presents in an organic and integral way the traditional content of God's revelation and the Christian message: creed, sacraments, commandments, and prayer and worship. These basic teachings form the cognitive objective of catechesis. The universal Church provides catechists with the essential Catholic doctrines to be transmitted. What are they?[17]

1. The reality of God, as creator and giver of life (divinity); as Father, who loves and cares for each individual (Providence); as the one and only source of eternal happiness (eschatology).

2. The Mystery of Christ:
   the Son of God who became one of us (incarnation);
   the Liberator who can free us from all obstacles to become what we were created to be: children of God (salvation);
   the Teacher who taught us the way to live (Gospels);
   the Lord who gave his life that we may live (paschal mystery);
   the Judge who will come again in glory (eschatology).

3. The action of the Holy Spirit, who unites God's people (Church); who makes us holy through sign and symbol (sacraments); who enables us to live and act like Christ (conscience);

[17]Francis J. Buckley, S.J., "The Catechism of the Catholic Church: An Appraisal," *Horizons* 20 (no. 2, Fall 1993) 309.

who inspires us to pray with and in Christ (spirituality); who empowers us to create a better world for all (social responsibility).

4. The role of Mary and the communion of saints.
5. The world as created and redeemed, as the site of a cosmic struggle between good and evil; and the role of the Church in the world today.

Faith expresses itself in doctrine and love. To foster that faith through every stage of life expresses the mission of the Church to teach as Jesus did.

Conclusion: Essentials of Christian Experience

1. As *human* experience, it is always the interpreted experience of a consciously knowing (cognitive) and loving (affective) subject. As cognitive, it is not mindless; as affective, it is not coerced/violent. It entails a critically reflective mind and a committed heart engaged in a faith-interpretation of all human experience. It is an experience of human freedom that is both private and public, individual and social, interior and external.
2. As *historical* experience, it occurs in time and space, and is based on the historical revelation of Jesus Christ and his community of faith. It entails a faith-interpretation of the past, present, and future. It commemorates what God has accomplished in Jesus Christ as the fulfillment of God's promise to Abraham; and it looks forward to the second coming of the crucified and risen Lord of history. It is a faith-experience of God's intervention in human history *(magnalia Dei),* of God as the ultimate origin-ground-meaning/sense of human history. It is an experience of time as *kairos,* wherein God is present and active, as opposed to time as mere *chronos,* routine/repetition apart from God. It entails a freedom *from* bondage to the tedium of *chronos,* and a freedom *for* the joy of experiencing the Eternal Now in the *kairos* of the divine presence and self-giving love. It is the experience of what Luke calls the "now" or "today" of communion with God: "Today, I must stay at your home" (19:5); "Today, salvation has come to this

house'' (19:9); ''Today, you shall be with me in paradise'' (23:43). In terms of place, it is a faith-interpretation that occurs within particular linguistic and cultural contexts, within historical landscapes and/or townscapes.

3. As *ecclesial* experience, it entails sharing a common faith, liturgy/worship, Scriptures, doctrines/beliefs, tradition/history, laws, practice, structures/churches. The Holy Spirit of Jesus Christ and his Father is the common good of the ecclesial experience that unites Christians, that gives rise to their faith, worship/liturgy, Scriptures, doctrines/beliefs, and life as a community-communion.

4. As *Trinitarian* experience, it is an experience of the Father's love for the Beloved Son and of the Beloved Son's love for the Father. It is the experience of our being the beloved sons/daughters of God in the Beloved Son. As the beloved brothers/sisters of the Beloved Son, it is our sharing the Son's experience of loving the Father above all. Their Holy Spirit of Love for one another constitutes our Trinitarian experience of the Three Persons' love for one another and our love for one another in their love. Christian prayer is always a Trinitarian experience of the Holy Spirit of the Father and the Son, apart from whom we cannot pray. It is always a participation in the communion-community-communications of the Three Persons, in the Eternal Now of their Eternal Life/Love.

5. As *joyful* experience, it is always communion, communication, and community with the joyful Spirit of Happiness Itself. It is the experience of a joy which this world neither gives nor takes away from us, because it is our sharing in the Spirit that is the eternal joy of the Father and the Son. The Spirit is where it acts, and joy—a fruit of the Spirit—manifests where it is and what it does. The joy of Eternal Life/Love, even now, transforms our experience of time into *kairos,* God's time, the time of God's joy-giving visitation. Even now, we know something of Happiness Itself.

6. As an *eschatological* experience, it occurs within the tension of promise and fulfillment, the ''even-now and not-yet,'' as all creation yearns for the fullness of time, the complete manifestation of the consummation of the plan of God in

Christ. It is an experience of eschatological hope in the face of the incompleteness, partiality, evil, imperfection, and suffering that must be endured with loving patience before the second coming. It entails the hunger and thirst of the human spirit for God, who alone can satisfy it, as Goodness and Truth and Beauty Itself. The ultimate meaning of Christian experience is always beyond it/transcends it: "Eye has not seen, ear has not heard, nor has it so much as dawned on us what God has prepared for those who love Him" (1 Cor 2:9).

7. As *self-transcending* experience, it is always precarious. It entails the tension between the self as transcending in following the Beloved Son's way to the Father and the self as transcended. Christian experience is never some pure and serene possession. So we are bid to watch and pray, to make our way in fear and trembling, lest we lapse into a state of radical faithlessness, hopelessness, and lovelessness/self-will or godlessness.

8. As an *all-pervasive* experience, rooted in an abiding faith and hope and love, it is an apprehension of all reality that has a relative as well as an absolute aspect. It places all experienced reality in the light and the shadow of transcendent reality. In the shadow, for transcendent reality (God) is supreme and incomparable. In the light, for transcendent reality links itself to all other (created) reality to transform, magnify, and glorify it. Within the light of Christian faith and hope and love, all created reality becomes absorbed in the all-encompassing goodness of God, its Creator, Sustainer, and Destiny. The Blessed Trinity is the ultimate context within which all the Christian's experience finds its ultimate meaning and goodness.

7

Theology of Beauty: Résumé of Presuppositions

1. The triune God is Happiness Itself. God is identical with God's happiness.
2. The triune God is the One, True, Good, and Beautiful. These four transcendentals are conceptually distinct but ontologically identical and interchangeable with Being Itself/God.
3. The Four transcendentals are aspects of Happiness Itself.
4. Happiness Itself is an interpersonal unity of communion, community, and communications consisting of knowing its truth, loving its goodness, and delighting in the beauty of its truth and goodness.
5. The triune God, Happiness Itself, delights in its unity, truth, and goodness; It knows the truth of its unity, goodness, and beauty; it loves the goodness of its unity, truth, and beauty.
6. The triune God, Happiness Itself, is Spirit: the One, the True, the Good, and the Beautiful. All created/human happiness, unity, truth, goodness, and beauty is a limited participation in Happiness/Truth/Goodness/Beauty Itself or Spirit. Transcendentals are rooted in spirit (divine/human) as aspects of Being Itself.
7. The triune God, Happiness Itself, is the Common Good of the universe/all creation. There is no happiness, unity, truth, goodness or beauty apart from its origin-ground-fulfillment

in the Triune God, Happiness Itself, the Common Good of all creation.

8. The triune God, Goodness Itself, is the Common Good that originates, sustains, perfects, and fulfills all created/finite/human happiness, unity, truth, goodness, and beauty. All created goodness participates in the Common Good/Goodness Itself/Triune God. God is one, good, true, and beautiful by God's essence; creatures are so by participation. God alone exists by God's essence; creatures exist by participation. God is Being Itself; creatures receive or have it by participation.
9. God sees (knows) all that God has made, and it is good because God sees it and sees it as good. God's vision is not a response to created beauty/goodness; it is the cause of created beauty/goodness.
10. God creates all in God's likeness. The unity, truth, goodness, and beauty of creation reflects the Creator as the One, the True, the Good, and the Beautiful. The One creates a cosmos/universe rather than chaos, within which there is an order of interrelated, interacting, interdependent, parts enabling our affirmation of the unity, truth, goodness, and beauty of things.
11. The Spirit/God is where the Spirit/God acts. The Spirit/God acts as the principle of unity, truth, goodness, and beauty of all the universe/creation; as the Creator, Sustainer, Director, and Fulfillment of the universe/creation. The unity, truth, goodness, and beauty of things are, therefore, evidence of the presence and activity of the Spirit/God. The Spirit/God reveals something of Itself in creation.
12. Because God acts freely, both God's creation and revelation are gifts or forms of God's self-giving. God is in God's gifts, giving them existence, unity, truth, goodness, and beauty, as well as meaning, direction, and purpose. All creation is, therefore, a motive for gratitude. Nothing exists that we have not been freely/lovingly given. All creation irradiates the splendor of the Creator's self-giving love.
13. God is not an object to be known among other objects. No object/creature is self-explanatory. God is known as the tran-

scendent explanation for all objects/creatures. Similarly, nothing makes sense out of context. God is the Ultimate Context in and from which all objects/creation make sense or has sense/meaning/purpose. Being Itself, the One/True/Good/ Beautiful Itself, is the measure of all created reality which possesses existence and its transcendental qualities by participation. Apart from its Ultimate Context, all creation is ultimately absurd or meaningless.

14. The faith whereby we apprehend the splendor/beauty of transcendent Love-Wisdom has a relative as well as an absolute aspect; for it apprehends all things in the light and shadow of that Love-Wisdom. In the shadow, for transcendent Love-Wisdom is supreme and incomparable. In the light, for transcendent Love-Wisdom transforms, magnifies, and glorifies all things within its all-encompassing goodness. The triune God, Truth/Goodness/ Beauty Itself, is not a part of creation; rather, God transforms, magnifies, and glorifies it.

15. God created the universe, as Thomas affirms (*In Div. Nom.*, c. 4, lect. 5, n. 349), to make it beautiful for himself by reflecting his own beauty. Out of love for the beauty of his own true goodness, God gives existence to everything, and moves and conserves everything. Beauty Itself intends everything to become beautiful within the fullness of its own true goodness.

16. We reflect Beauty Itself to the extent that we conform to it. We become beautiful in conforming to the grace and call of God's will/love/truth for us. Self-will, in opposition to God, deforms our God-given beauty; for we are true in God's truth, good in God's goodness, and beautiful in the beauty of God's true goodness.

17. Just as there is a distinction between our true good and an apparent good, there is a distinction between true beauty and seductive beauty. True beauty, like our true good, is whatever attracts us to our true fulfillment and happiness. Seductive beauty entails whatever allures us to our self-destruction (morally or spiritually). The same distinction holds between the prudent and the clever person. Although both have a talent for knowing the means to achieve their ends, the former is moral (virtuous) and the latter is immoral. Similarly, there

are true solutions and pseudo-solutions to problems. There are true friends and apparent friends.

18. True beauty entails our true joy/delight in knowing and loving things as they truly are: God above all, and everything else as limited. There is no true joy/delight in loving God for less than what God is or in loving a creature above all. True love and joy entail loving things as they truly are. Our true happiness is always related to our true knowledge and love of true beauty and goodness. Self-deception can never ground such joy or happiness.

19. As the perfect image of God, Jesus Christ is perfectly conformed to God as the Incarnate Word/Light/Love/Beauty of the triune God's Eternal Word/Light/Love/Beauty. He is the transfigured and transfiguring Son of Man and Son of God, transforming/transfiguring the deformed image and likeness of God in self-willed humankind. He is the communion of the divine and human creating communion/community/communications between God and humankind. He is the sacrament of God, the efficacious sign, making all things beautiful in the beauty of God's true love and goodness. Jesus Christ and his Church are the sacrament for the triune God's making all things beautiful, for reforming/transforming/conforming/transfiguring the deformed/disfigured/distorted human image of God in order that all humankind might have life fully in communion/community/communications with Truth/Goodness/Beauty Itself.

20. Our Christian faith apprehension of the glory/beauty of God in Jesus Christ, the beauty of the Incarnate Word/Light/Love, results from the Triune God's gift of God's Holy Spirit. It is our loving knowing and knowing loving that results from God's showing his love for us by the gift of God's Spirit to our hearts (Rom 5:5). It is the knowledge-born-of-love, of the mutual love that unites Father, Son, and Christian. Without faith, without the eye of love, we cannot joy in the beauty of love visible in Christ, who "reflects the glory of God" (Heb 1:3). Such faith enables Paul to see God working in all things for the good of those who love him (Rom 8:28). It enables us to see the beauty of God's loving kindness in all things. Hearts can, however, grow cold; we can lose sight of

God's loving kindness. God gives God's self to us in all our experience, whether or not we have the eye of love to see the beauty of God's self-giving love.

21. God's creating the universe to be beautiful implies that God creates it to be delightful; for the beautiful is delightful. Because God is Happiness/Beauty Itself, our conformity to God entails our participation in Happiness/Beauty Itself. "Thy will be done" implies our welcoming Happiness/Beauty Itself. God's will for us is always God's true love and happiness for us. The triune God, Happiness/Beauty Itself, is eternally and essentially self-giving. Our happiness and beauty, therefore, consist in accepting/welcoming/participating in God's self-giving Spirit. We can contemplate Beauty Itself in persons manifesting the splendor of God's self-giving Spirit. God's beauty is manifested wherever God's will is done because God's will for us is always God's love for us. Beauty is the splendor of God's love. It is the radiant joy of Happiness/Love/Truth Itself.

22. Salvation in Jesus Christ means freedom *from* and freedom *for*. Jesus is God's servant Messiah sent to free us from *all* the obstacles to our having communion, community, and communication with Happiness/Truth/Love/Beauty Itself. Jesus Christ and his Church are the triune God's saving sacrament (efficacious sign) freeing humankind *for* communion, community, and communication with Happiness/Truth/Love/Beauty Itself. Jesus Christ and his Church are the sacrament Happiness/Truth/Love/Beauty Itself for the beauty and joy of all creation. The triune God is operative in the sacramental liturgy of the Church for the beauty and joy of humankind under the sovereignty of God's eternal and invincible love.

23. The beauty of God's love in Jesus Christ manifests the good news of our Way to the Truth and Life of Happiness Itself.

24. Catholic doctrines of the universal Church ground a Catholic theology of beauty.

    Creation. All creation reflects the beauty of its knowing and loving Creator; therefore, we can contemplate something of Beauty Itself in all creation.

Providence. Having created all things to be beautiful, the Creator draws them to the ultimate perfection of their beauty in eternal communion-community-communication with Beauty Itself.

Eschatology. The beatific vision of Beauty Itself is the destiny and eternal happiness of all who love God. "Eye has not seen, nor ear heard . . . what God has prepared for those who love him."

Incarnation and *Revelation.* Jesus Christ is the incarnate Son and revelation of God/Beauty Itself.

Christology. Jesus Christ is the perfect image/form of God because he is perfectly conformed to the mind and heart of God.

Soteriology. Christ, the perfect form of God, transforms/transfigures/beautifies/divinizes/saves/redeems a sinful/deformed humankind as the Good/Beautiful Shepherd who, when lifted up in the mystery of the Cross, draws all humankind to himself/Beauty Itself incarnate. The self-giving power of Beauty/Love Itself saves the world.

Pneumatology. God's love poured into our hearts through the gift of the Spirit transforms us, enabling us to see with the eye of love/faith all things in the light of Beauty Itself. We rejoice even now in our faith/love vision that is a prelude to the beatific vision and eternal happiness.

Appendix 1

The Catechism and Beauty

The *Catechism of the Catholic Church* (Dublin: Veritas, 1994, p. 2500) gives considerable attention to the capacity of beauty to evoke a sense of the divine:

> The practice of goodness is accompanied by spontaneous spiritual joy and moral beauty. Likewise, truth carries with it the joy and splendour of spiritual beauty. Truth is beautiful in itself. Truth in words, the rational expression of the created and uncreated reality, is necessary to man, who is endowed with intellect. But truth can also find other complementary forms of human expression, above all when it is a matter of evoking what is beyond words: the depths of the human heart, the exaltation of the soul, the mystery of God. Even before revealing himself to man in words of truth, God reveals himself to him through the universal language of creation, the work of his Word, of his wisdom: the order and harmony of the cosmos—which both the child and the scientist discover—"from the greatness and beauty of created things comes a corresponding perception of their Creator," "for the author of beauty created them" (Wis 13:3, 5).

The *Catechism* (p. 32) quotes St. Augustine about beauty:

> Question the beauty of the earth, question the beauty of the sea, question the beauty of the air distending and diffusing itself, question the beauty of the sky . . . question all these realities. All respond: "See, we are beautiful." Their beauty is a profession *(confessio)*. These beauties are subject to change. Who made them if not the Beautiful One *(Pulcher)* who is not subject to change?

The *Catechism* calls attention to the beauty and love visible in Christ, attaching great importance to the symbolism in the mysteries of the life of Jesus and to the symbolic forms under which the Holy Spirit has been made known to us. The symbolism of baptism, for example, is conveyed by the following passage (*Catechism,* p. 1216) from St. Gregory of Nazianzus:

> Baptism is God's most beautiful and magnificent gift. . . . It is called *gift* because it is conferred on those who bring nothing of their own; *grace* since it is given even to the guilty; *Baptism* because sin is buried in the water; *anointing* for it is priestly and royal as are those who are anointed; *enlightenment* because it radiates light; *clothing* since it veils our shame; *bath* because it washes; and *seal* as it is our guard and the sign of God's Lordship.

The *Catechism* (p. 1162) invokes St. John Damascene as a witness to the way in which the beauty of holy images can assist Christian prayer and contemplation. The *Catechism* (p. 1156) affirms that "beauty expressive of prayer" should characterize liturgical song and music. It underscores (p. 2502) the beautiful harmony and efficacy of liturgical signs in the life of the faithful:

> . . . the contemplation of sacred icons, united with meditation on the Word of God and the singing of liturgical hymns, enters into the harmony of the signs of celebration so that the mystery celebrated is imprinted in the heart's memory and is then expressed in the new life of the faithful.

The *Catechism* (p. 2500) reminds us that truth is beautiful in itself; it carries with it the joy and splendor of spiritual beauty. As sovereign truth, God alone fully satisfies the mind's quest for explanation and meaning. In giving us intelligence and a capacity for truth, God orders us to himself. The added light of revelation assists the mind to escape from its own darkness (pp. 2466, 2470).

Goodness, which ranks with beauty and truth as the third transcendental, is the attractiveness and beneficence of being. As the fullness of being, God is supremely lovable and loving. Creation is attributed to the generosity of divine love, which wills to share its own goodness (pp. 356–58). The supreme calling of every human being is to love God in return and to live according to the law of love. All the commandments of God and of the Church are traced back to the twofold precept of love, which Jesus himself quoted from the Jewish Torah. The core of Christian morality is the new law of the gospel, infused into human hearts by the Holy Spirit. Christ is in his own person the way of perfection (p. 1952).

Appendix 2

The Good/True/Beautiful Known Analogously

Bernard Lonergan, in his Cincinnati lectures of 1959 on the philosophy of education, spoke of the human good as object. His explanation of our analogous knowledge of the human good is equally applicable to our analogous knowledge of beauty. His explanation that follows is taken from Robert M. Doran and Frederick E. Crowe, eds. *Collected Works of Bernard Lonergan: Topics in Education,* ch. 2, "The Human Good as Object: Its Invariant Structure" (Toronto: University of Toronto Press, 1993) 30–32.

> I have said a number of things that the good is not. It is not abstract, not an aspect, not a negation, not just a double negation, not merely ideal, not apart from evil, and not static. Then what is it? You recall the passage in the Gospel where the young man said to our Lord, "Good Master," and our Lord replied, "Why do you call me good? One alone is good" (Mark 10:17). There is a pregnant sense of the word "good" in which One alone is good. According to St. Thomas there is a strong sense of the Aristotelian *ti esti, quid sit?* what is it? that refers to a full understanding of the object. When you ask, "What is the good?" in that sense, you are asking, "What is good by its essence?" "What is good" asks for the essence, and there is only one thing that is good by its essence, and that is God. Everything else is good by participation; just as there is only one thing that exists by its essence, and everything else exists by participation. That good, that being, is known properly, as opposed to analogously, only in the beatific vision. You know what is the good, what is being, by its essence, when you have beatific vision. Otherwise you know them only analo-

gously. In other words, one must attend not merely to the analogous concepts but also to analogous knowledge. Analogous knowledge is what is really important. Our knowledge of being and the good, like our knowledge of God, is analogous, because God alone is and is good by his essence. You cannot know the good by its essence unless what is good by its essence is the object. The only knowledge you can have of being or of the good through beings by participation is an analogous knowledge. Consequently, as one's knowledge of finite beings and finite goods becomes more full, more perfect, more adequate, in the same proportion one has a fuller, more adequate, more perfect basis for forming an analogous notion of what the good is.

Perhaps this will help us see what lies behind the profound contrast between Plato and Aristotle. In the *Republic* Plato wants to find out what the good man would be, and seeks to answer this question by describing the good society. At the term of the argument, he says that, if the good society is to exist, the guardians will have to know the Idea of the good. Knowing the Idea of the good is the ultimate solution to all human problems. But Aristotle said in his *Ethics* that whatever may be the case with regard to the Idea of the good, obviously it cannot make much difference to the goodness of concrete human living. That is a matter of acquiring the right habits. Aristotle studies things in the concrete.

Now there is a sense in which both Plato and Aristotle are correct. The Idea of the good really is God himself. The divine essence is the essence of the good, and the *only* essence of the good, the only place where the essence of the good is found. And that is the measure of all other good. And the good is mysterious because God is mysterious. As Isaiah says, "My thoughts are above your thoughts, and my ways are above your ways" (Isa 55:8). On the other hand, anything that exists and is good by participation is finite, and because it is finite it is not perfect in every respect; it can be criticized. The possibility of noting that it is not good in every respect, that it can be criticized, is for St. Thomas the basis of human freedom. One cannot choose between God and anything else, but one can always choose between finite things, because they are finite in their being and in their goodness. They are not good from every possible viewpoint. Criticism is possible. Hence one can say that what is beyond criticism is either God or an idol, because the finite good is always open to criticism. The possibility of finding fault, of seeing that something is not perfect in every respect, is the basis of liberty. . . . But the finite good cannot be treated as though it were infinite and as though it were beyond criticism, and to treat it as though it were beyond criticism is to set up an idol.

The Notion of the Beautiful: A Paraphrasing of Lonergan's "The Notion of the Good"

Philosophy speaks of the good, the true, and the beautiful as transcendentals. Being and the transcendentals are convertible. The good/true/beautiful exists, and what exists is good/true/beautiful. The beautiful is not an abstract notion. It is comprehensive. It includes everything. When you speak of the beautiful, you do not mean some aspect of things, as though the rest of their reality were ugly. The beautiful is a notion that is absolutely universal, that applies to whatever exists and at the same time is totally concrete. That is what I mean by saying it is a comprehensive term. When we use the word "concrete," for example, the concept behind that word is not abstract. We are not talking about an abstraction when we talk about the concrete. As concepts, "abstract" and "concrete" seem to be quite the same. Yet we are talking about an abstraction when we use the word "abstract," but that is not so when we talk about the concrete. There are different types of terms, then, and terms like "concrete," "good," "beautiful," "being," are comprehensive. So our first point about the beautiful is that it is comprehensive, and hence not abstract.

The beautiful, like the other transcendentals, is not an aspect. The definition of the beautiful is *id quod visum placet,* what delights the eye. However, it is not only *what* delights that is beautiful; the capacity to see and to delight, and the seeing and the delighting, no less than having the concrete situation in which the seeing and delighting in the beautiful can occur, is also constitutive of our enjoying the beautiful. So one can see that not only what is seen is beautiful, but also the seeing and the delighting, the capacity to see and to delight; and all the skills that go into the process of fulfillment, and the fulfillment itself are beautiful. The definition of the beautiful does not exhaust the notion of the beautiful. What everyone delights in seeing is certainly beautiful, but there is a whole set of other elements that are related to it, and they are beautiful, too.

The beautiful is not negative. It is more than the absence of ugliness, of unattractiveness. Furthermore, the beautiful is not merely an ideal. The beautiful and the ugly are in things. The ideal is relevant to the beautiful insofar as the existing beauty is incomplete and in the process of completion. The beautiful is not an ideal that does not exist and is beyond possible attainment. The beautiful is the concrete, and the ideal is the next stage in the development of the concrete.

Just as the good is not apart from evil in this life, the beautiful is not apart from ugliness. God could have created a world without evil or ugliness, but thought it better to permit both and draw good and beauty out of them. We must not forget that what God wants—the world God foreknew from all eternity in all its details and freely chosen according to God's infinite wisdom and infinite goodness—is precisely the world in which we live, with all its details and all its aspects. This is what gives meaning to the phrase that might at times be considered trite: resignation to the will of God. God does not will any sin, either directly or indirectly. God wills only indirectly any privation or punishment. What God wills directly is the good and the beautiful, and that alone. Yet the good/beautiful that God wills and freely chooses with infinite wisdom and infinite goodness is this world. It is good/beautiful, then, that is not apart from evil/ugliness. It is a good/beauty that comes out of evil/ugliness, that triumphs over both.

The beautiful/good is not static. It is not the fulfillment of some blueprint. We develop. We are intelligent, and successive ages learn something more. St. Thomas's proof that beatitude cannot be had in this life is that beatitude is rooted in intellectual perfection, and no one in this life knows so much that later generations cannot discover something more; consequently, the only people who could have beatitude, if beatitude lay in this life, would be the last generation. Moreover, the good and the beautiful in this world come out of evils and ugliness, and that coming out is another dynamic aspect of the good/beautiful in this world.

The beautiful/good is known analogously. If we have said that the good/beautiful is not abstract—not an aspect, not a negation, not merely an ideal, not apart from evil, and not static—then what is it? We recall the passage where the young man in the gospel said to Jesus, "Good Master," and Jesus replied, "Why do you call me good? God alone is good'' (Mark 10:17). There is a sense of the word ''good'' (and likewise ''beautiful'') in which God alone is good. When we ask, ''What is good/beautiful'' with reference to a full understanding of the object, we are asking, ''What is good/beautiful by its essence?'' There is only one reality that is good/beautiful by its essence, and that is God. Everything else is good/beautiful by participation; just as there is only one thing that exists by its essence, and everything else exists by participation. That good/beautiful, that being, is known properly, as opposed to analogously, only in the beatific vision. You know what is the good/beautiful, what is being, by its essence, when you have the beatific vision. Otherwise you know them only analogously. Our knowledge of being and the good/beautiful, like our knowledge of God, is analogous, because God alone is and is good/beautiful by essence. You cannot know the good/beautiful by its essence unless what is good/beautiful by its essence is the object. The only knowledge you can have of being or of the good/beautiful through beings by participation is an analogous knowledge. Consequently, as our knowledge of finite beings and finite goods/beauty becomes fuller, more perfect, more adequate, in the same proportion we have a fuller, more adequate, more perfect basis for forming an analogous notion of what the good/beautiful is.

Goodness/Beauty Itself is the measure of all other good/beauty. And the good/beauty is mysterious because God is mysterious. As Isaiah says, ''My thoughts are above your thoughts, and my ways are above your ways'' (55:8). On the other hand, anything that exists and is good/beautiful by participation is finite, and because it is finite it is not perfect in every respect; it can be criticized. The possibility of noting that it is not good/beautiful in every respect, that it can be criticized, is for St. Thomas the basis of human freedom. One cannot choose between God and anything else, but one can always choose between finite things, because they are finite in their being and in their goodness/beauty. They are not good/beautiful from every possible viewpoint. Criticism is possible. Hence one can say that what is beyond criticism is either God or an idol, because the finite good/beauty is always open to criticism. The possibility of finding fault, of seeing that something is not perfect in every respect, is the basis of liberty.

The finite good/beauty cannot be treated as though it were infinite and as though it were beyond criticism, and to treat it as though it were beyond the criticism is to set up an idol.